FOR ORGANS, PIANOS & ELECTRONIC KEYBOARDS

**E-Z PLAY TODAY**

**73**

# MICHAEL JACKSON

Cover photo by Phil Dent / Contributor / Getty Images

ISBN 978-1-4950-9768-3

**HAL•LEONARD®**

Visit Hal Leonard Online at
**www.halleonard.com**

Contact us:
**Hal Leonard**
7777 West Bluemound Road
Milwaukee, WI 53213
Email: info@halleonard.com

In Europe, contact:
**Hal Leonard Europe Limited**
42 Wigmore Street
Marylebone, London, W1U 2RN
Email: info@halleonardeurope.com

In Australia, contact:
**Hal Leonard Australia Pty. Ltd.**
4 Lentara Court
Cheltenham, Victoria, 3192 Australia
Email: info@halleonard.com.au

# Registration Guide

- Match the Registration number on the song to the corresponding numbered category below. Select and activate an instrumental sound available on your instrument.

- Choose an automatic rhythm appropriate to the mood and style of the song. (Consult your Owner's Guide for proper operation of automatic rhythm features.)

- Adjust the tempo and volume controls to comfortable settings.

## Registration

| 1 | Mellow | Flutes, Clarinet, Oboe, Flugel Horn, Trombone, French Horn, Organ Flutes |
|---|---|---|
| 2 | Ensemble | Brass Section, Sax Section, Wind Ensemble, Full Organ, Theater Organ |
| 3 | Strings | Violin, Viola, Cello, Fiddle, String Ensemble, Pizzicato, Organ Strings |
| 4 | Guitars | Acoustic/Electric Guitars, Banjo, Mandolin, Dulcimer, Ukulele, Hawaiian Guitar |
| 5 | Mallets | Vibraphone, Marimba, Xylophone, Steel Drums, Bells, Celesta, Chimes |
| 6 | Liturgical | Pipe Organ, Hand Bells, Vocal Ensemble, Choir, Organ Flutes |
| 7 | Bright | Saxophones, Trumpet, Mute Trumpet, Synth Leads, Jazz/Gospel Organs |
| 8 | Piano | Piano, Electric Piano, Honky Tonk Piano, Harpsichord, Clavi |
| 9 | Novelty | Melodic Percussion, Wah Trumpet, Synth, Whistle, Kazoo, Perc. Organ |
| 10 | Bellows | Accordion, French Accordion, Mussette, Harmonica, Pump Organ, Bagpipes |

# Bad

Registration 7
Rhythm: Rock

Words and Music by
Michael Jackson

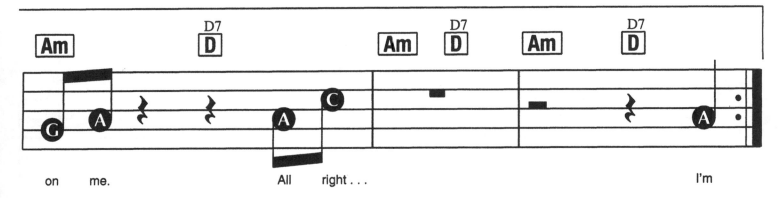

on me.     All   right . . .                                    I'm

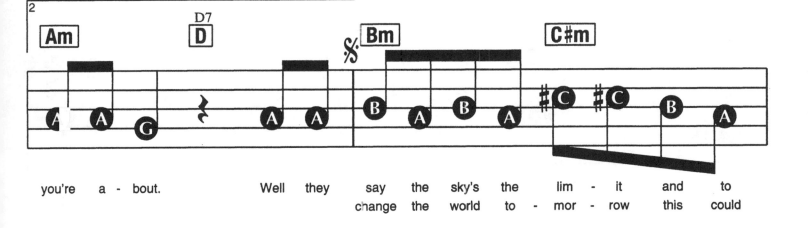

you're a - bout.     Well  they   say   the  sky's   the  lim - it   and   to
                     change the world  to - mor - row  this  could

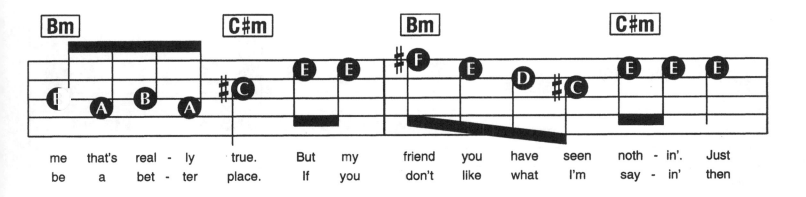

me   that's  real - ly   true.    But   my   friend   you   have  seen  noth - in'.  Just
be    a    bet - ter   place.    If   you   don't   like   what   I'm   say - in'  then

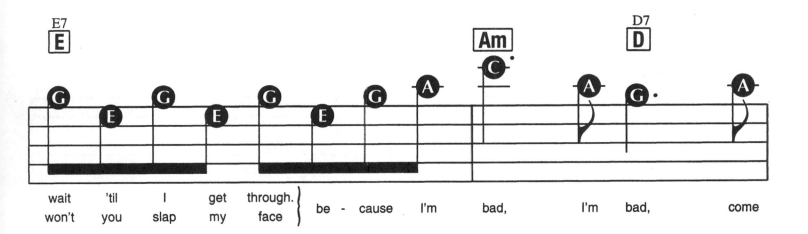

wait   'til    I    get  through.  be - cause   I'm   bad,      I'm   bad,     come
won't  you   slap   my   face

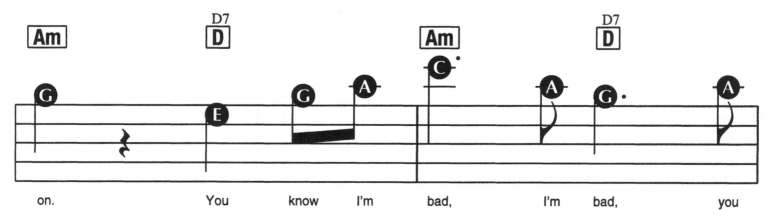

on. You know I'm bad, I'm bad, you

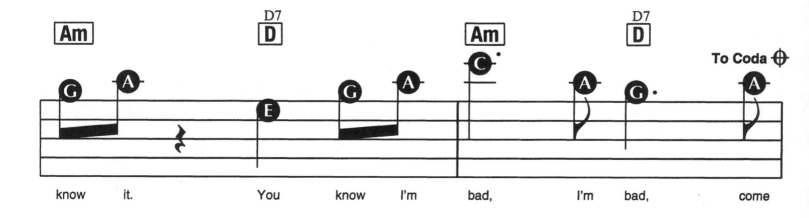

know it. You know I'm bad, I'm bad, come

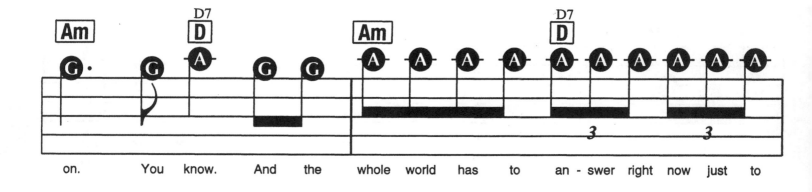

on. You know. And the whole world has to an-swer right now just to

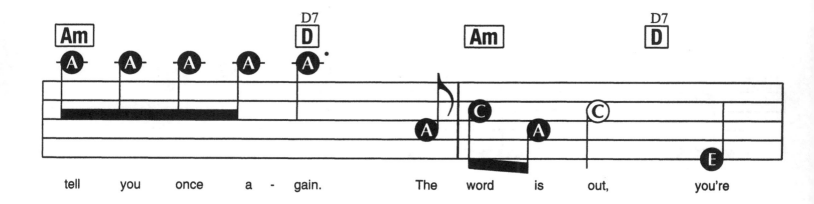

tell you once a-gain. The word is out, you're

7

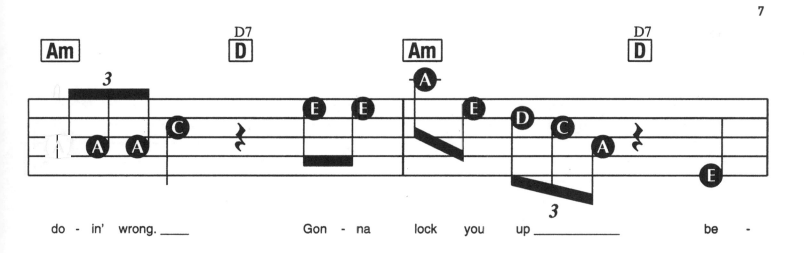

do - in' wrong. ____ Gon - na lock you up ____ be -

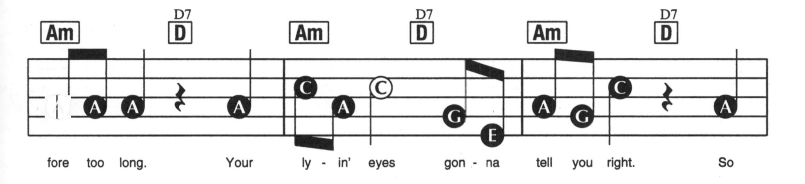

fore too long. Your ly - in' eyes gon - na tell you right. So

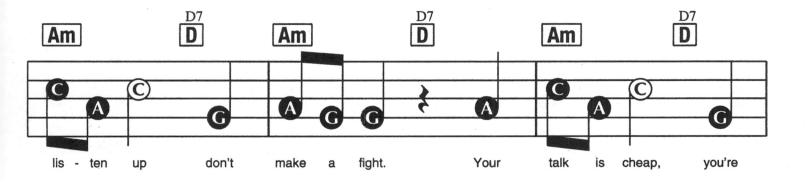

lis - ten up don't make a fight. Your talk is cheap, you're

**D.S. al Coda**
(Return to 𝄋
Play to ⊕ and
Skip to Coda)

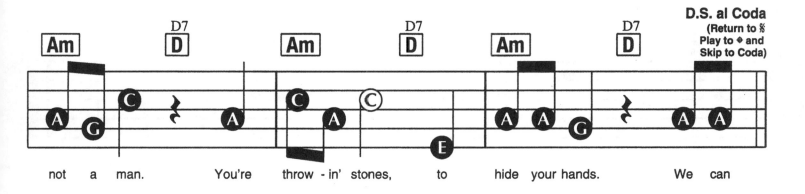

not a man. You're throw - in' stones, to hide your hands. We can

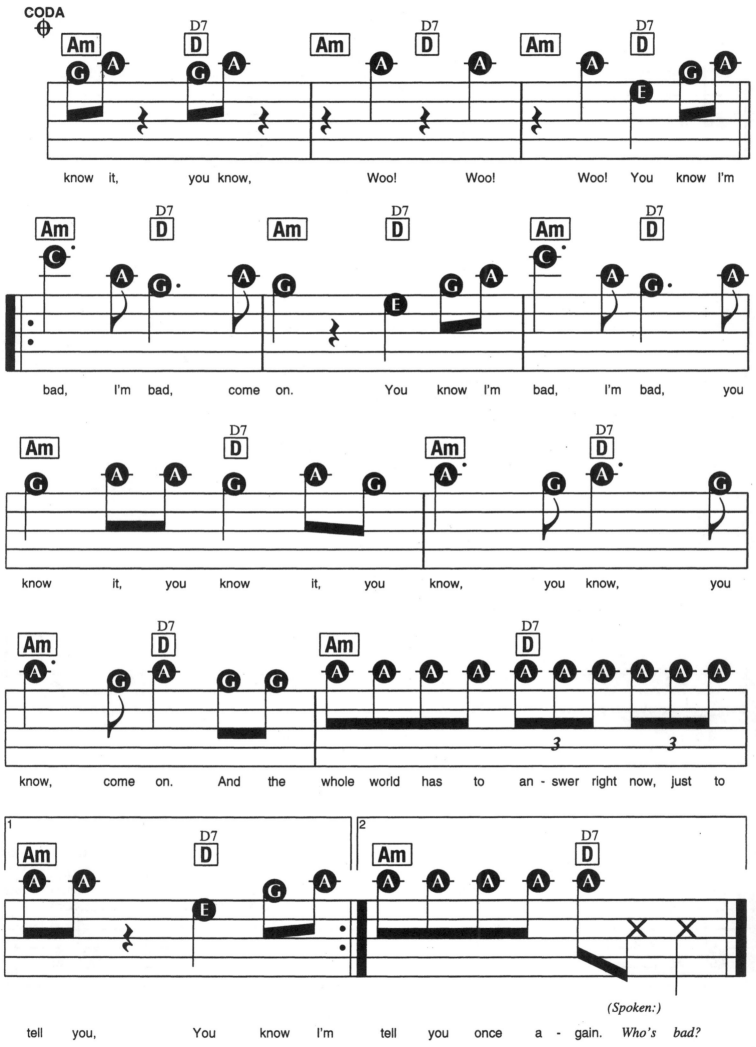

CODA

know it,      you know,          Woo!       Woo!          Woo! You     know I'm

bad,      I'm bad,     come on.          You   know I'm   bad,      I'm bad,      you

know      it,     you    know      it,      you    know,      you know,      you

know,     come on.     And    the    whole    world    has    to    an - swer right now, just to

tell    you,          You    know I'm    tell    you    once    a - gain. Who's  bad?

(Spoken:)

# Beat It

Registration 7
Rhythm: Rock

Words and Music by
Michael Jackson

They told him, "Don't you ev - er come a - round here. Don't
They're out to get you. Bet - ter leave while you can. Don't

wan - na see your face; you bet - ter dis - ap - pear." The
wan - na be a boy; you wan - na be a man. You

fire's ____ in their eyes and their words are real - ly clear. So
wan - na stay a - live; bet - ter do what you ____ can. So

beat it, just beat it.
beat it, just beat it.

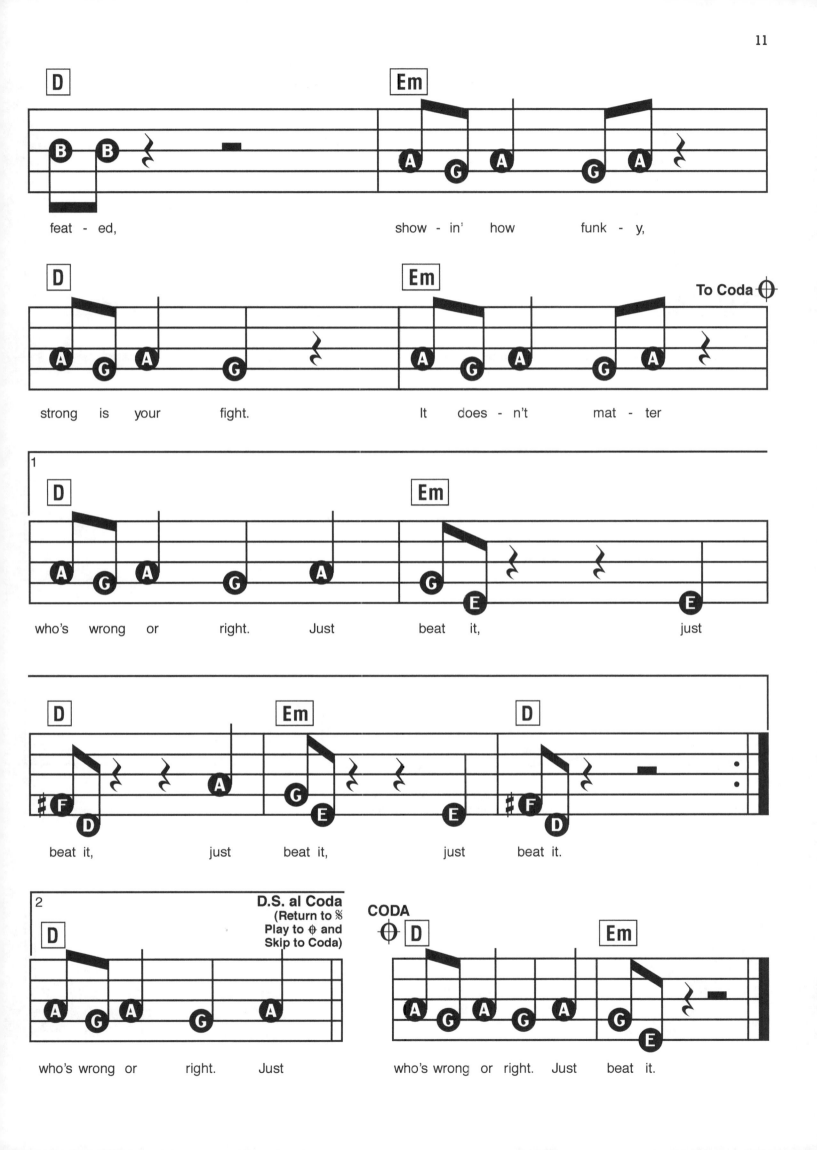

# Billie Jean

Registration 4
Rhythm: Rock

Words and Music by
Michael Jackson

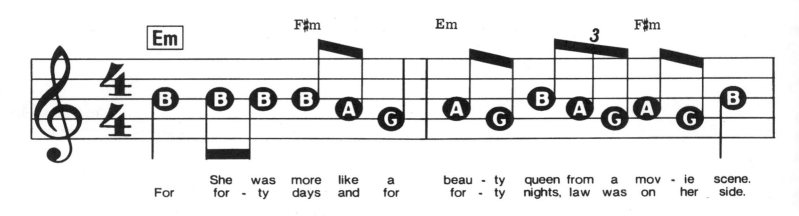

For
She was more like a beau - ty queen from a mov - ie scene.
for - ty days and for for - ty nights, law was on her side.

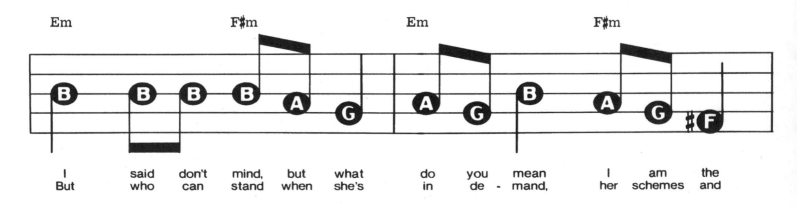

I said don't mind, but what do you mean I am the
But who can stand when she's in de - mand, her schemes and

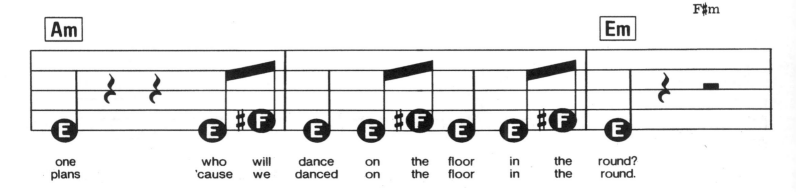

one who will dance on the floor in the round?
plans 'cause we danced on the floor in the round.

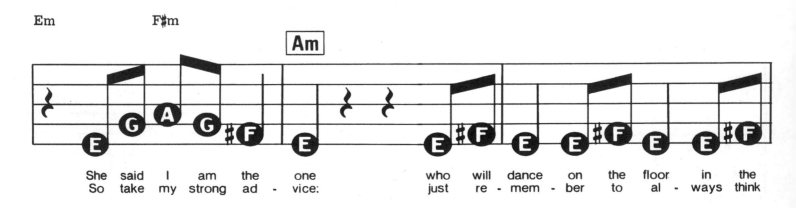

She said I am the one who will dance on the floor in the
So take my strong ad - vice: just re - mem - ber to al - ways think

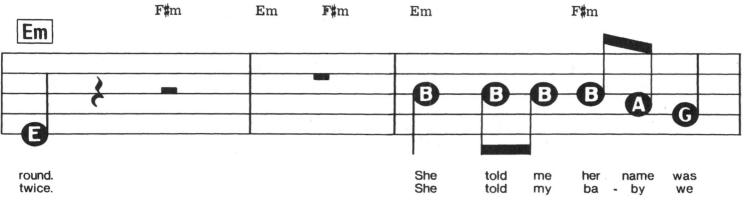

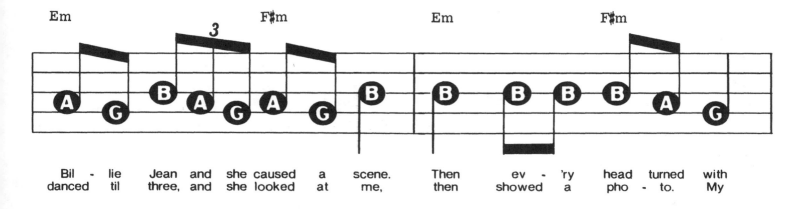

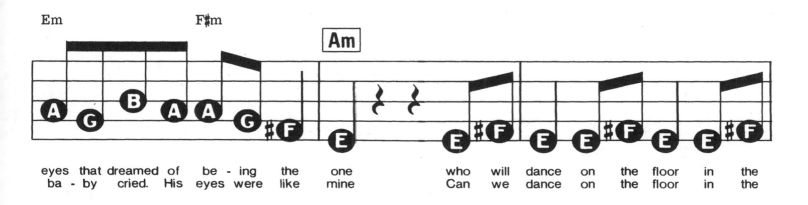

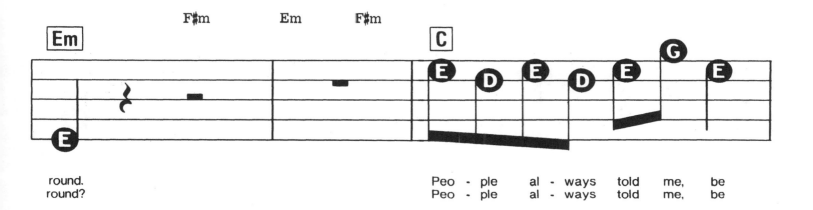

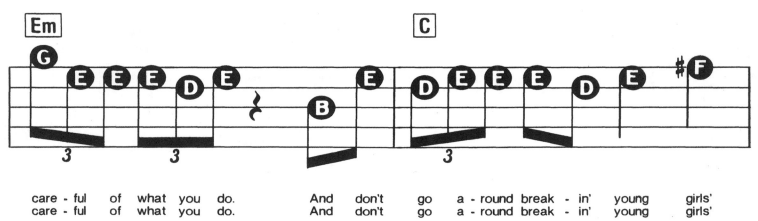

care - ful of what you do. And don't go a - round break - in' young girls'
care - ful of what you do. And don't go a - round break - in' young girls'

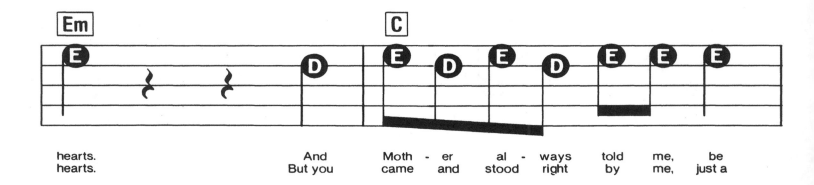

hearts. And Moth - er al - ways told me, be
hearts. But you came and stood right by me, just a

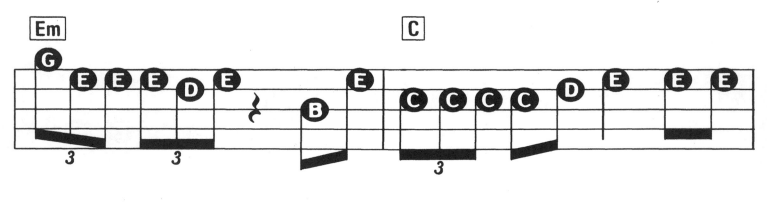

care - ful of who you love. And be care - ful of what you do. 'cause the
smell of sweet ____ per - fume. This hap - pened much ____ too soon. She _____

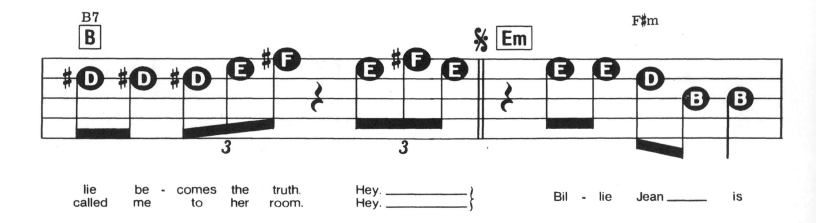

lie be - comes the truth. Hey. _____ Bil - lie Jean _____ is
called me to her room. Hey. _____

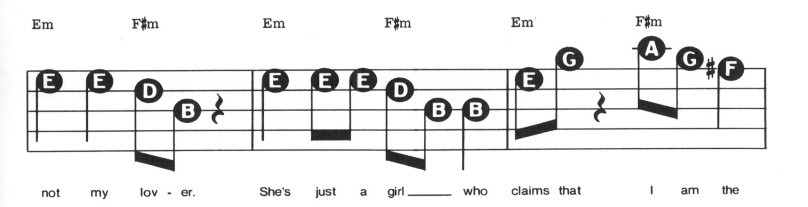

not my lov - er. She's just a girl _____ who claims that I am the

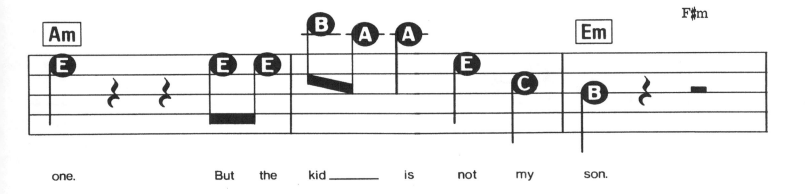

one. But the kid _____ is not my son.

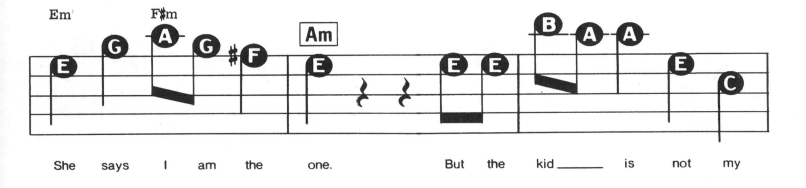

She says I am the one. But the kid _____ is not my

son.

# Black or White
## (Rap Version)

Registration 4
Rhythm: Rock or 8-Beat

Words and Music by Michael Jackson
Rap Lyrics by Bill Bottrell

17

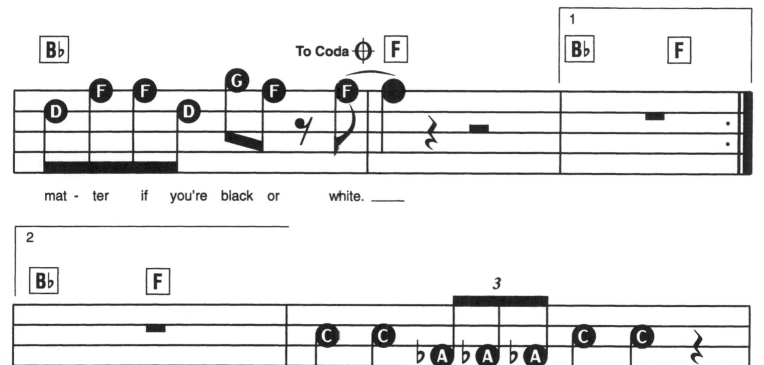

mat - ter  if  you're  black  or  white. ____

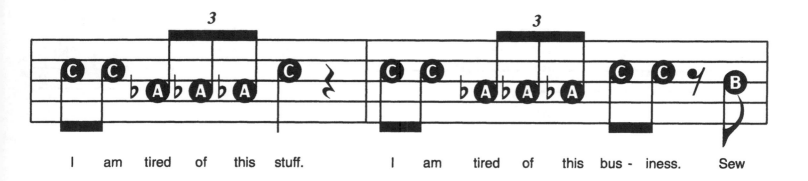

I  am  tired  of  this  dev - il.

I  am  tired  of  this  stuff.    I  am  tired  of  this  bus - iness.    Sew

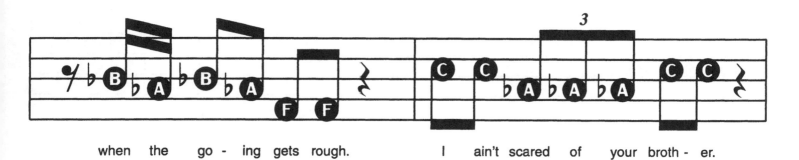

when  the  go - ing  gets  rough.    I  ain't  scared  of  your  broth - er.

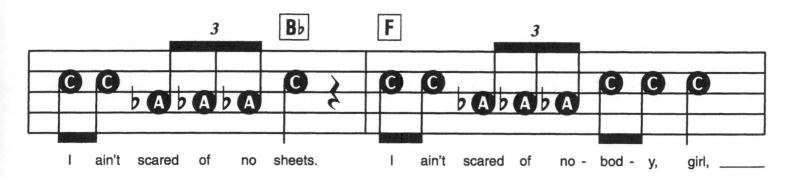

I  ain't  scared  of  no  sheets.    I  ain't  scared  of  no - bod - y,  girl, ____

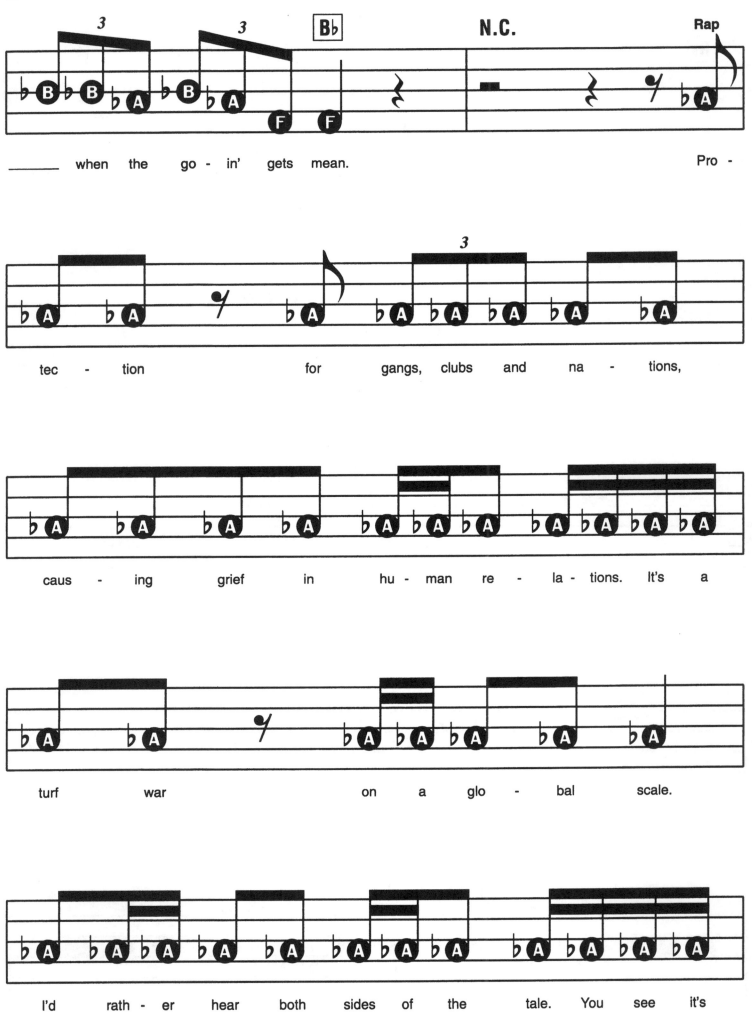

_____ when the go - in' gets mean.                                    Pro -

tec - tion                    for    gangs,   clubs   and    na - tions,

caus - ing    grief    in    hu - man    re - la - tions.    It's    a

turf    war                on    a    glo - bal    scale.

I'd    rath - er    hear    both    sides    of    the    tale.    You    see    it's

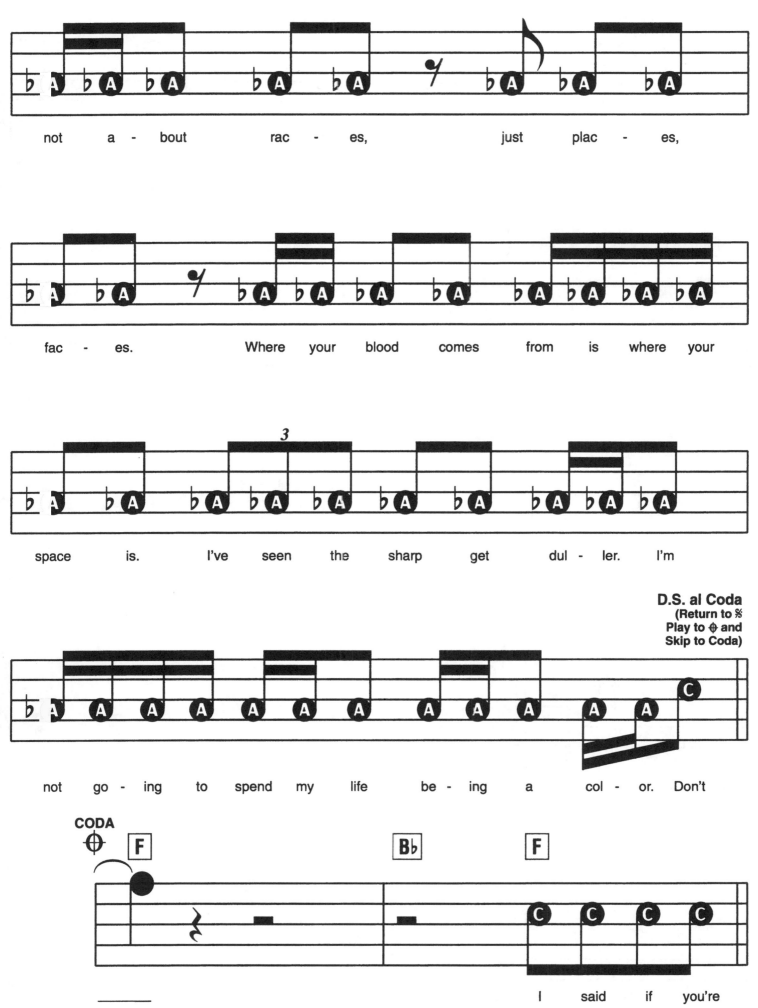

not a - bout rac - es, just plac - es,

fac - es. Where your blood comes from is where your

space is. I've seen the sharp get dul - ler. I'm

**D.S. al Coda**
**(Return to %**
**Play to ⊕ and**
**Skip to Coda)**

not go - ing to spend my life be - ing a col - or. Don't

**CODA**

**F**  **B♭**  **F**

_____ I said if you're

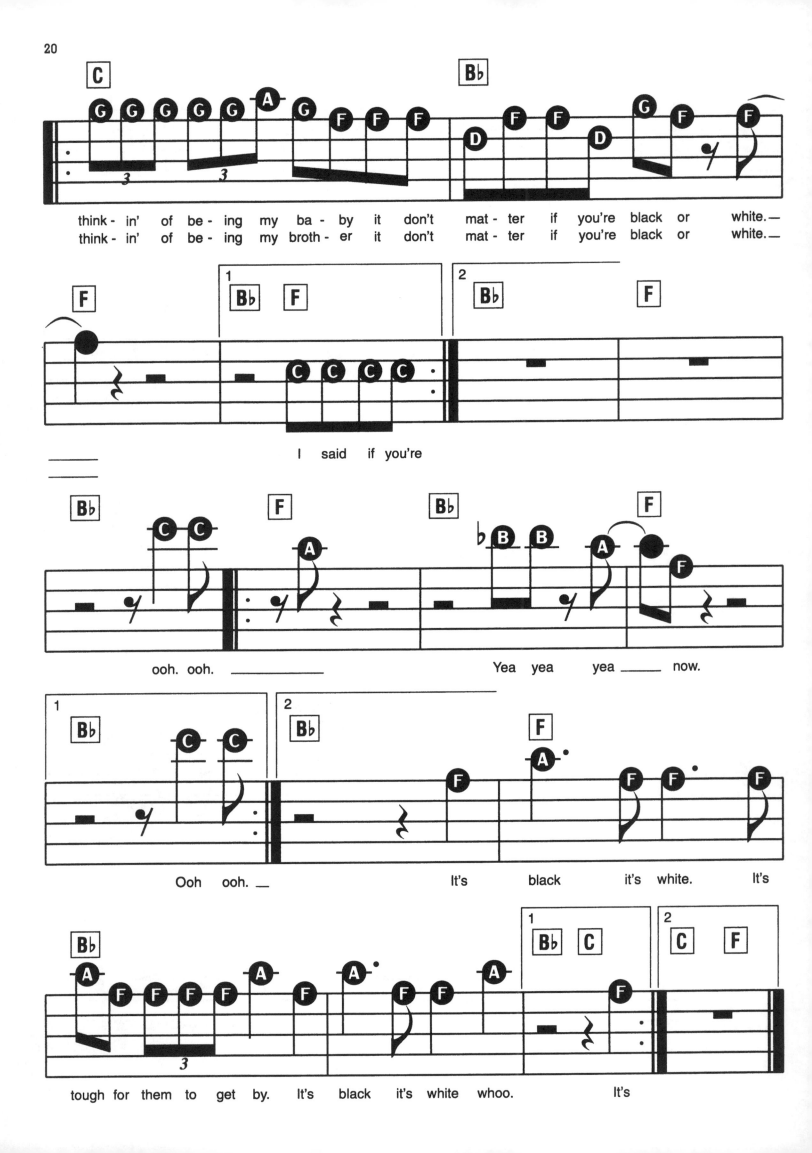

# Don't Stop Till You Get Enough

Registration 9
Rhythm: Rock or Disco

Words and Music by
Michael Jackson

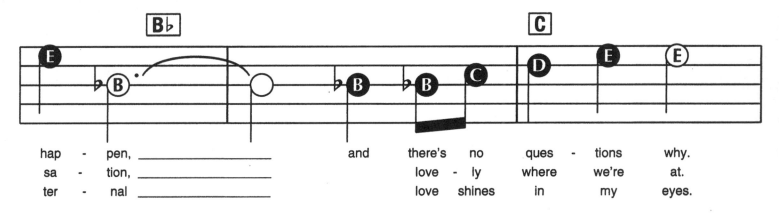

hap - pen, _____ and there's no ques - tions why.
sa - tion, _____ love - ly where we're at.
ter - nal _____ love shines in my eyes.

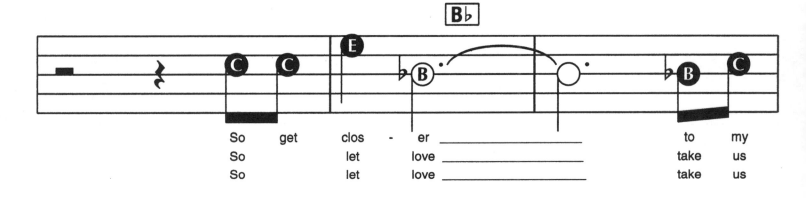

So get clos - er _____ to my
So let love _____ take us
So let love _____ take us

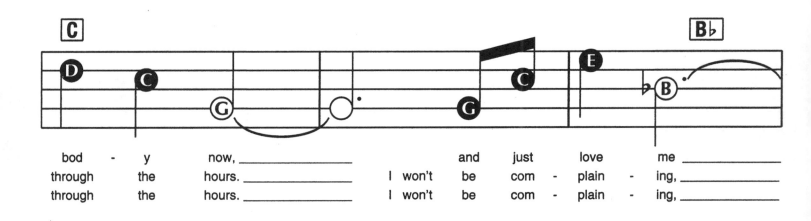

bod - y now, _____ and just love me _____
through the hours. _____ I won't be com - plain - ing, _____
through the hours. _____ I won't be com - plain - ing, _____

_____ 'til you don't know how. _____
_____ this is love pow -
_____ this is love pow -

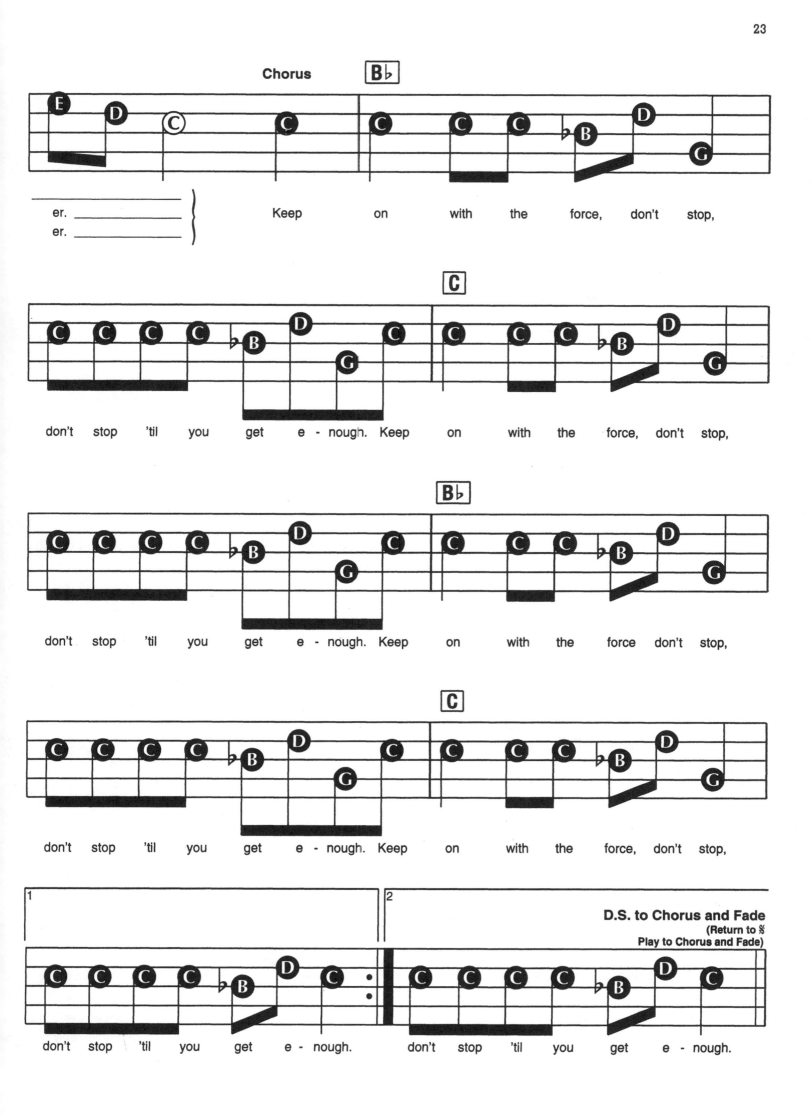

# Dirty Diana

Registration 5
Rhythm: Rock

Words and Music by
Michael Jackson

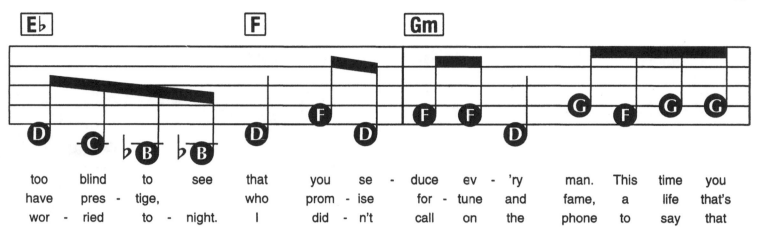

too | blind | to | see | that | you | se - | duce | ev - | 'ry | man. This | time | you
have | pres - | tige, | | who | prom - | ise | for - | tune | and | fame, a | life | that's
wor - | ried | to - | night. | I | did - | n't | call | on | the | phone | to | say that

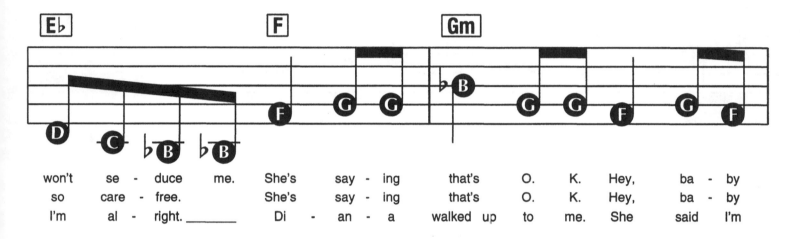

won't | se - | duce | me. | She's | say - | ing | | that's | O. | K. | Hey, | ba - | by
so | care - | free. | | She's | say - | ing | | that's | O. | K. | Hey, | ba - | by
I'm | al - | right. _____ | | Di - | an - | a | | walked | up | to | me. | She | said | I'm

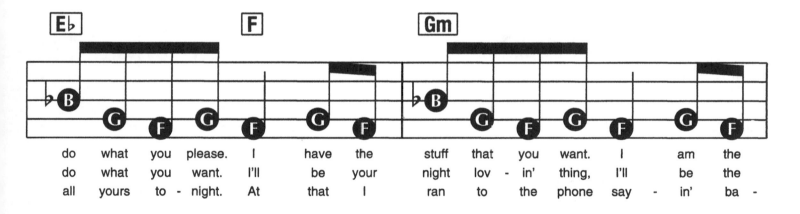

do | what | you | please. | I | have | the | stuff | that | you | want. | I | am | the
do | what | you | want. | I'll | be | your | night | lov - | in' | thing, | I'll | be | the
all | yours | to - | night. | At | that | I | ran | to | the | phone | say - | in' | ba -

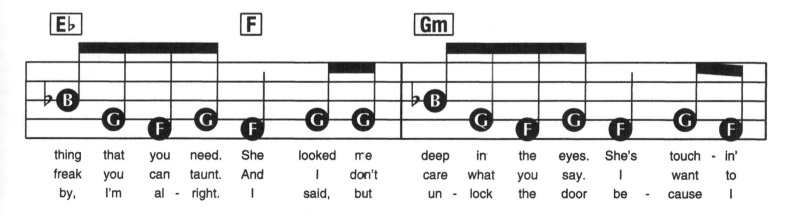

thing | that | you | need. | She | looked | me | deep | in | the | eyes. | She's | touch - | in'
freak | you | can | taunt. | And | I | don't | care | what | you | say. | I | want | to
by, | I'm | al - | right. | I | said, | but | un - | lock | the | door | be - | cause | I

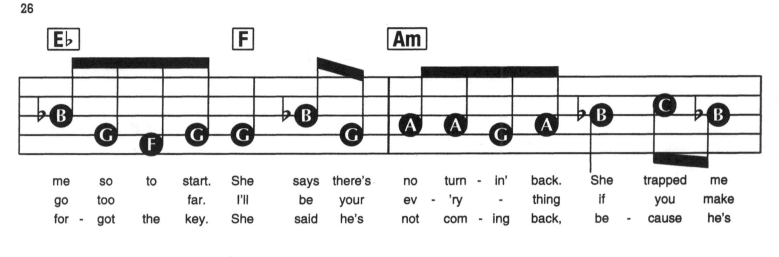

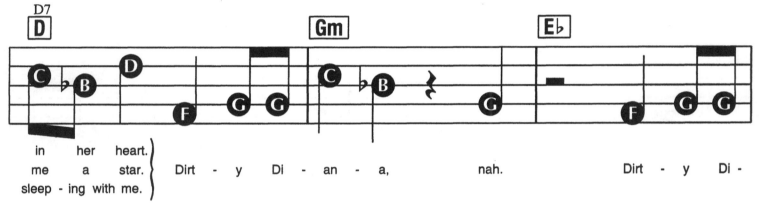

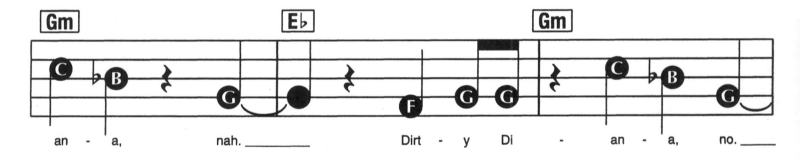

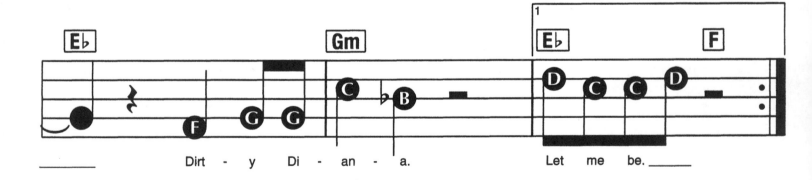

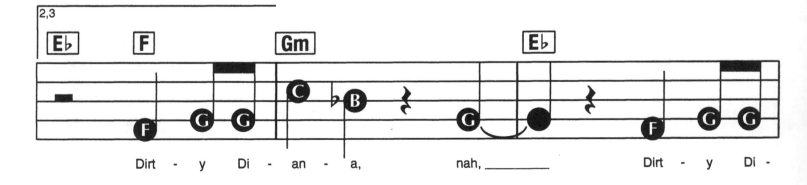

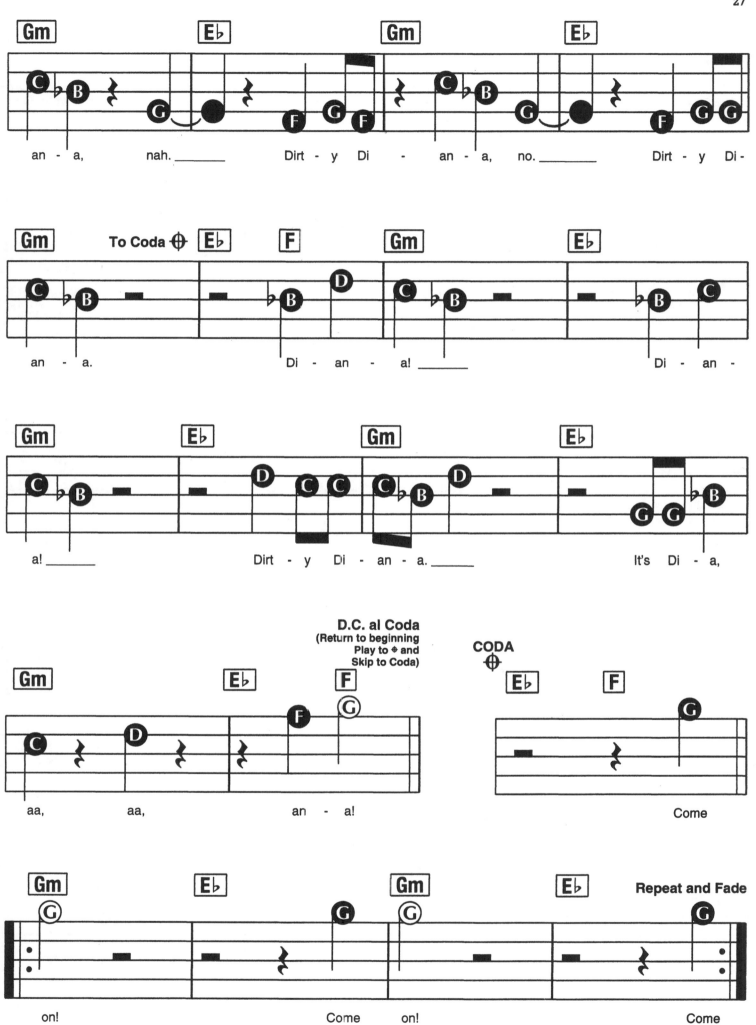

# The Girl Is Mine

Registration 1
Rhythm: Ballad or Pops

Words and Music by
Michael Jackson

29

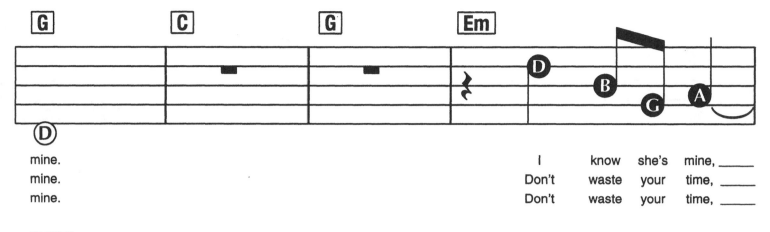

**G**      **C**      **G**      **Em**

mine.              I    know   she's   mine, _____

mine.          Don't   waste   your   time, _____

mine.          Don't   waste   your   time, _____

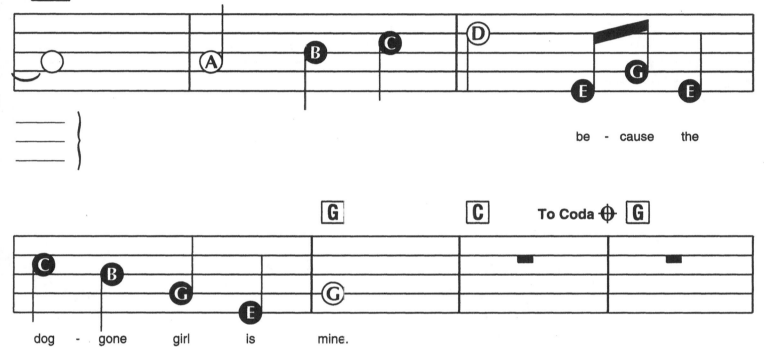

**Am**

be - cause    the

**G**      **C**    To Coda ⊕ **G**

dog - gone   girl   is   mine.

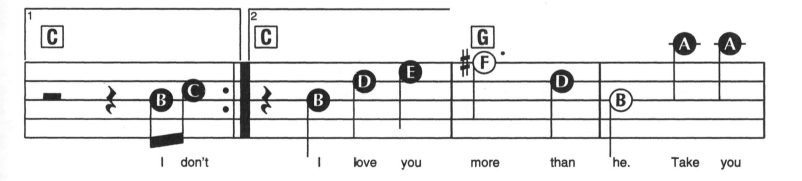

1. **C**      2. **C**      **G**

     I don't      I   love   you   more   than   he.   Take   you

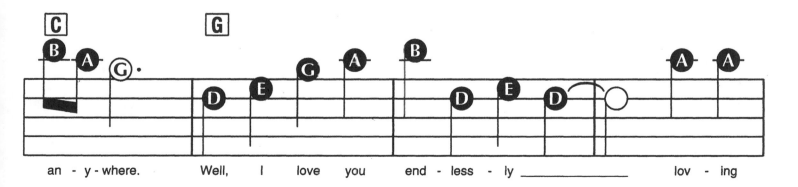

**C**      **G**

an - y - where.   Well,   I   love   you   end - less - ly _____   lov - ing

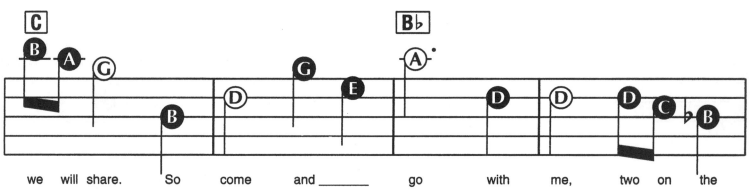

we will share. So come and _____ go with me, two on the

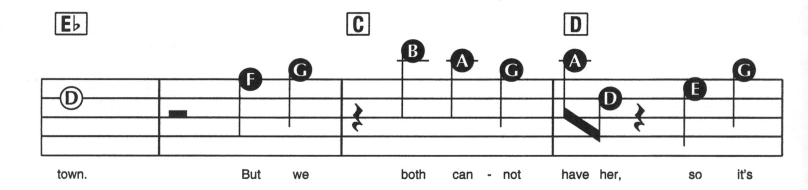

town. But we both can - not have her, so it's

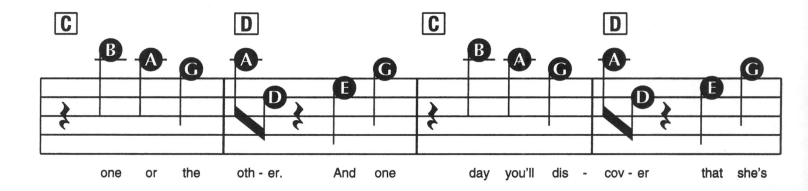

one or the oth - er. And one day you'll dis - cov - er that she's

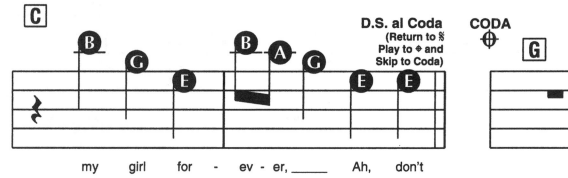

**D.S. al Coda**
(Return to % Play to ✛ and Skip to Coda)

**CODA**

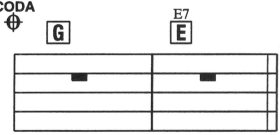

my girl for - ev - er, _____ Ah, don't

**Repeat and Fade**

# Man in the Mirror

Registration 5
Rhythm: Rock

Words and Music by Glen Ballard
and Siedah Garrett

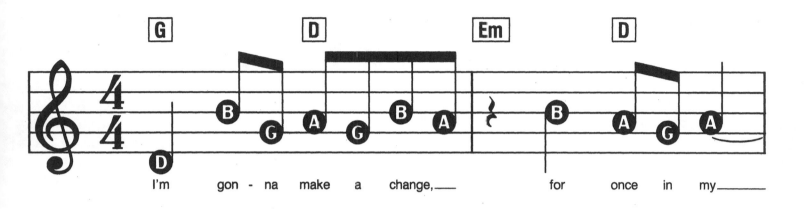

I'm gon - na make a change,___ for once in my___

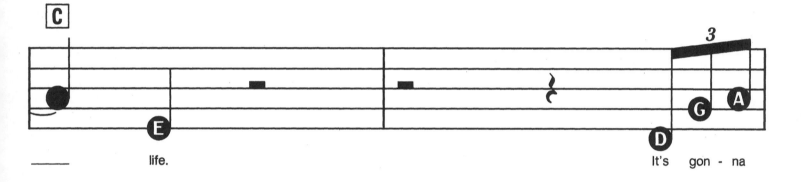

___ life. It's gon - na

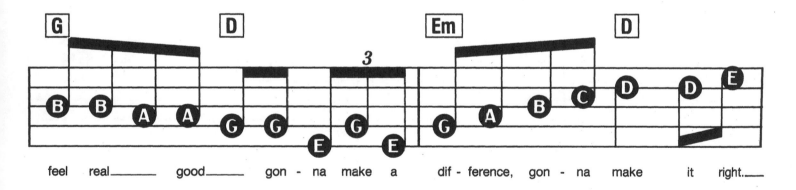

feel real___ good___ gon - na make a dif - ference, gon - na make it right.___

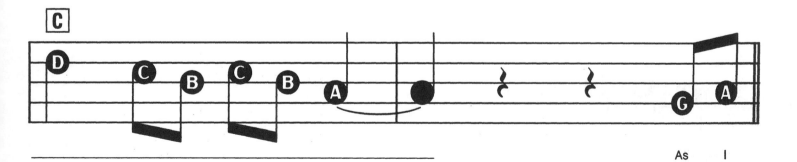

As I

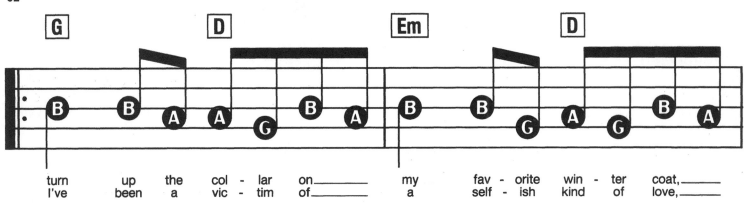

turn up the col - lar on_____ my fav - orite win - ter coat,_____
I've been a vic - tim of_____ a self - ish kind of love,_____

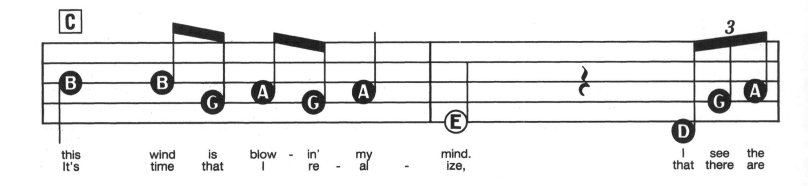

this wind is blow - in' my mind. I see the
It's time that I re - al - ize, that there are

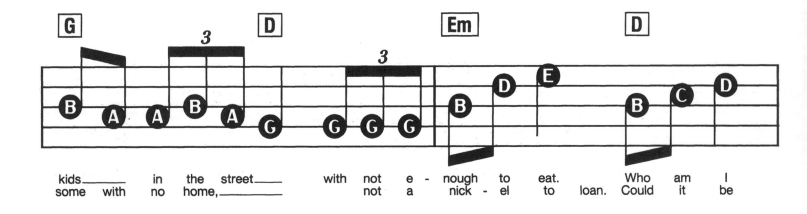

kids_____ in the street_____ with not e - nough to eat. Who am I
some with no home,_____ not a nick - el to loan. Could it be

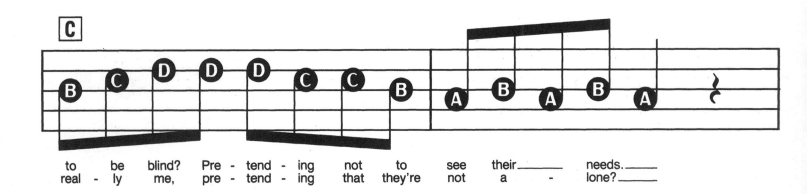

to be blind? Pre - tend - ing not to see their_____ needs._____
real - ly me, pre - tend - ing not that they're not a - lone?_____

33

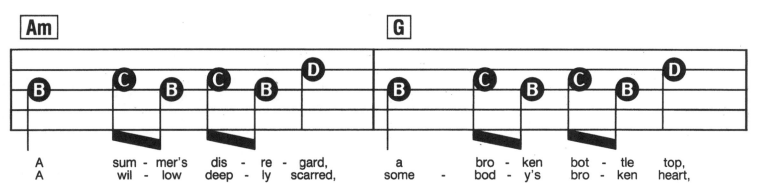

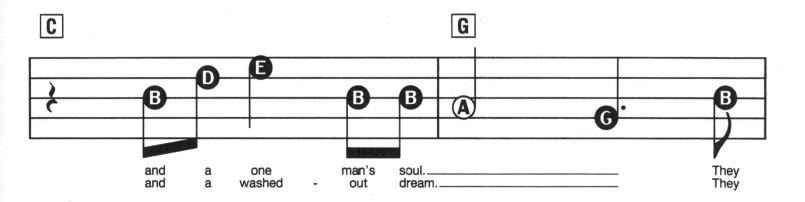

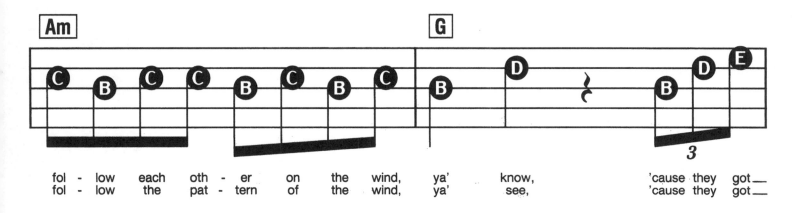

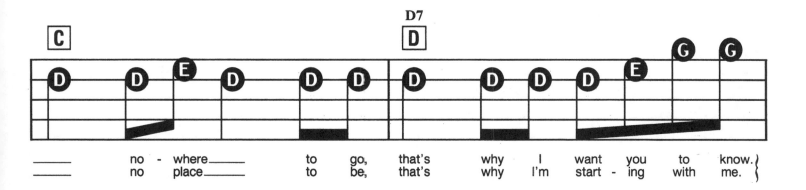

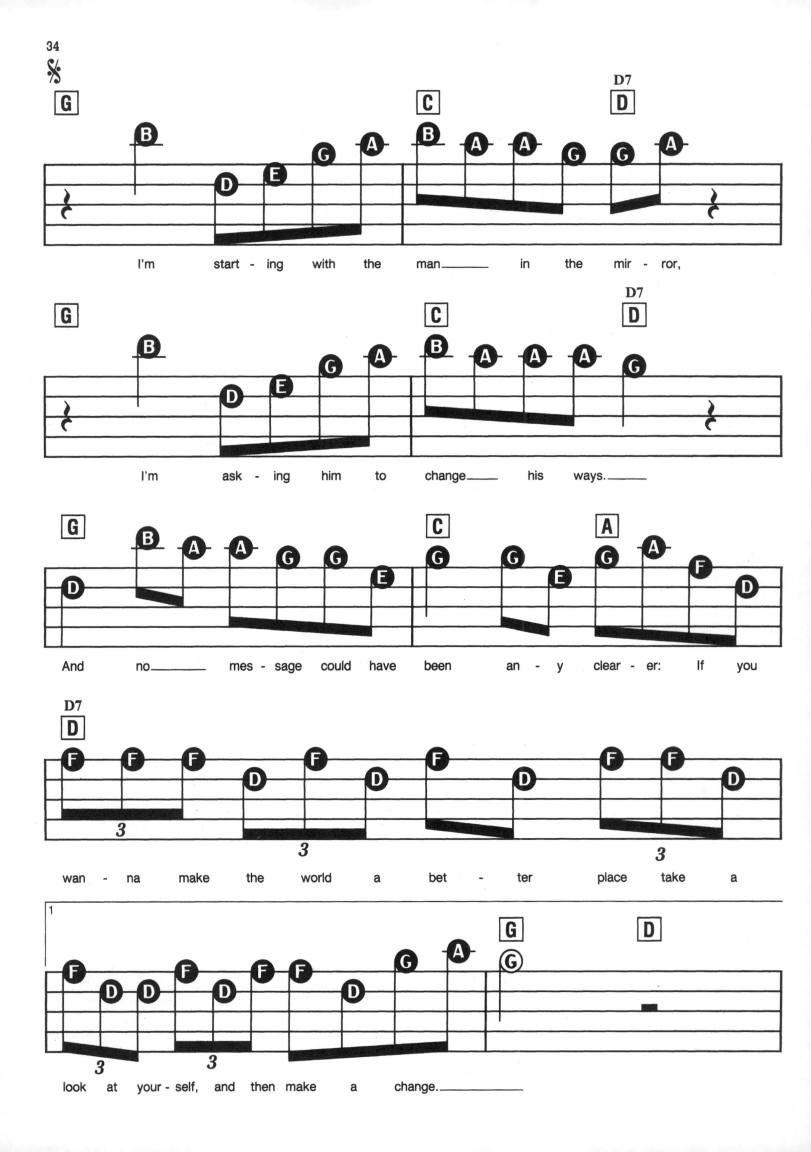

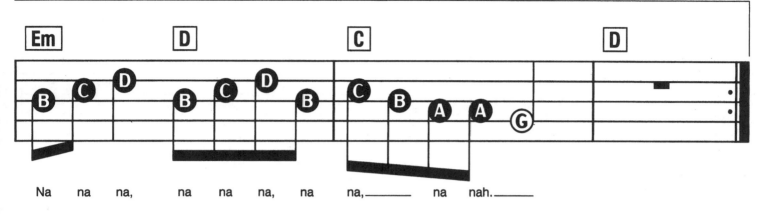

Na na na, na na na, na na,_____ na nah._____

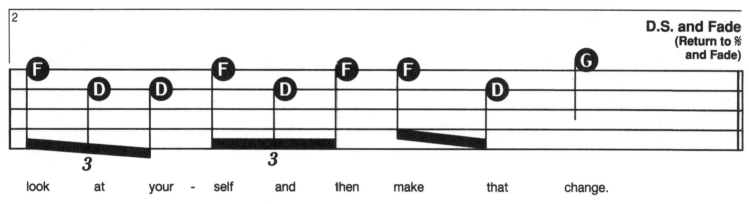

**D.S. and Fade**
(Return to 𝄋
and Fade)

look at your-self and then make that change.

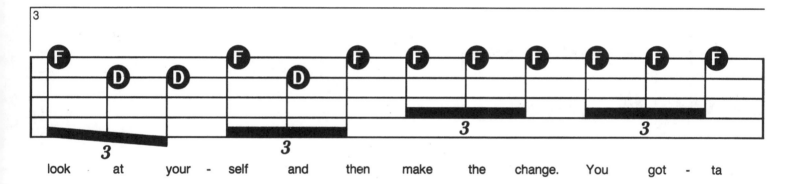

look at your-self and then make the change. You got-ta

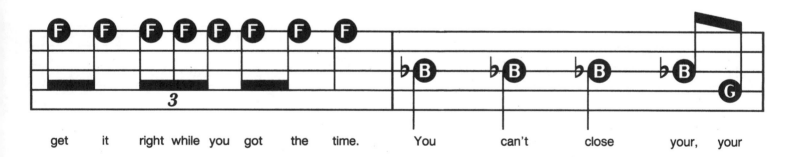

get it right while you got the time. You can't close your, your

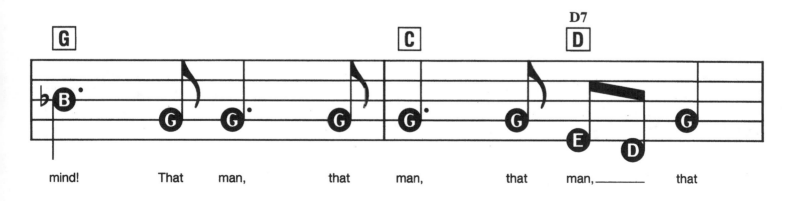

mind! That man, that man, that man,_____ that

good! Come on! Just lift your-

self, you know. You've got to stop it. Your-

self! I've got to make that change, to - day! Hoo!

You got to, you got to not let your-

self, broth - er. Hoo! *Spoken: Make that change.*

# Human Nature

Registration 10
Rhythm: Ballad or Pops

Words and Music by
John Bettis and Steve Porcaro

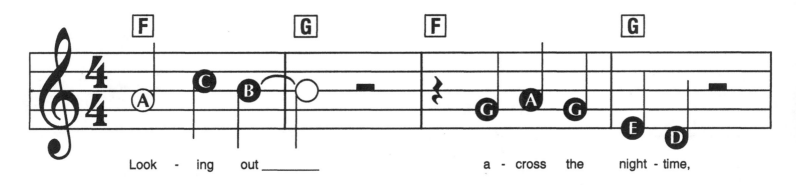

Look - ing out _____ a - cross the night - time,

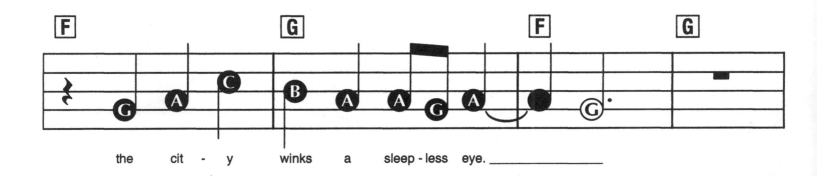

the cit - y winks a sleep - less eye. _____

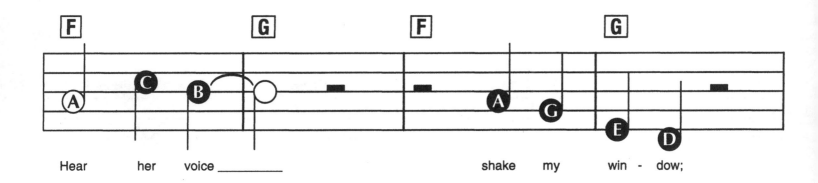

Hear her voice _____ shake my win - dow;

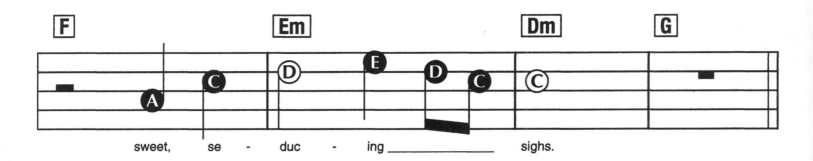

sweet, se - duc - ing _____ sighs.

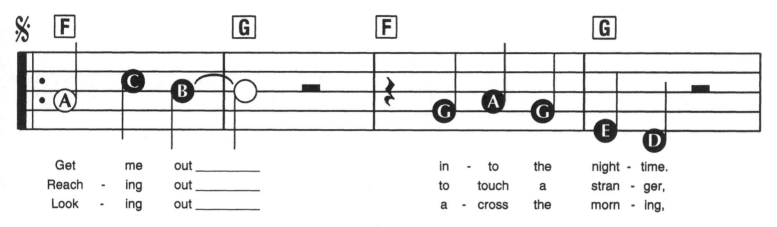

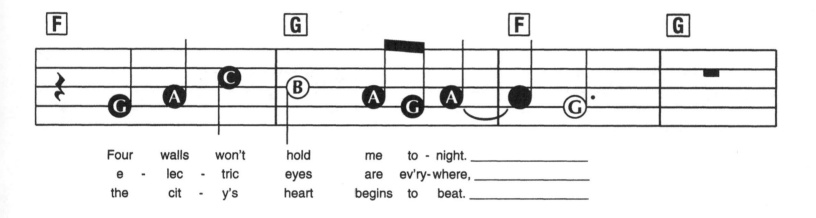

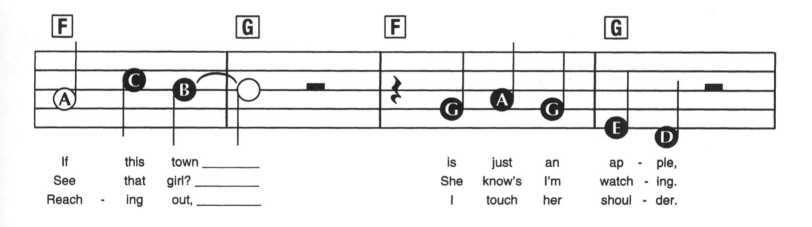

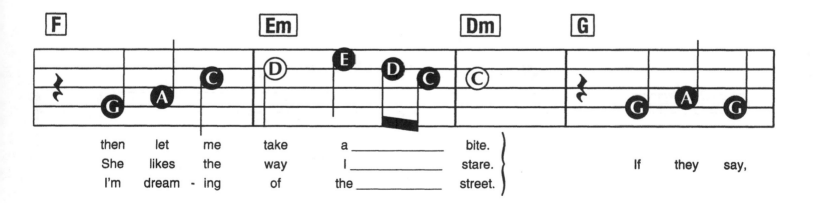

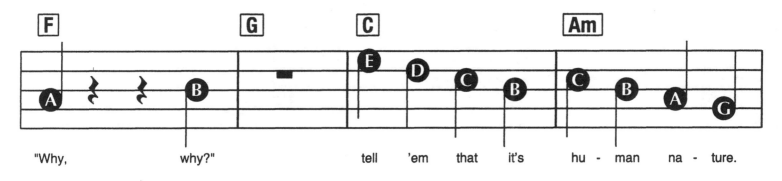

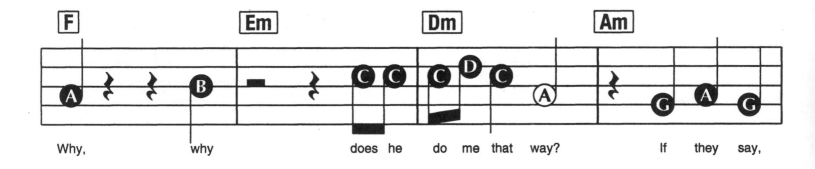

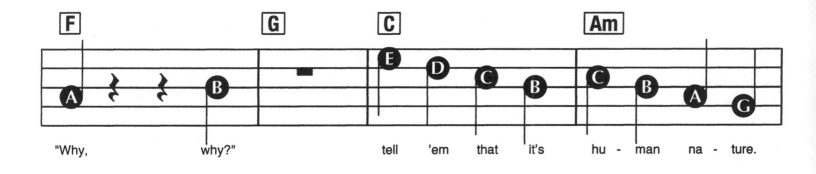

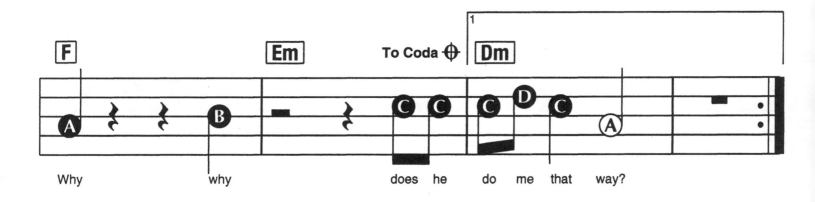

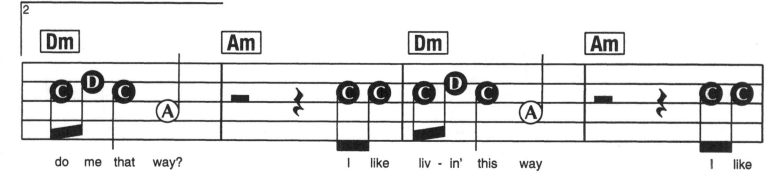

do me that way?   I like liv-in' this way   I like

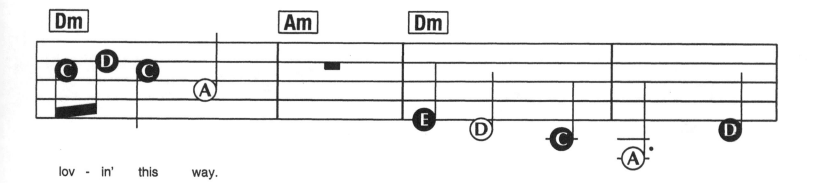

lov-in' this way.

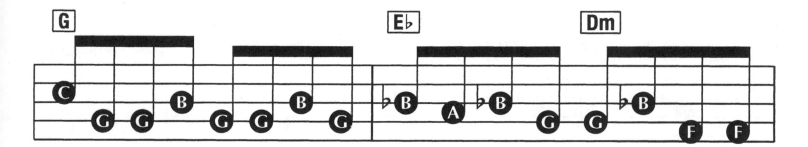

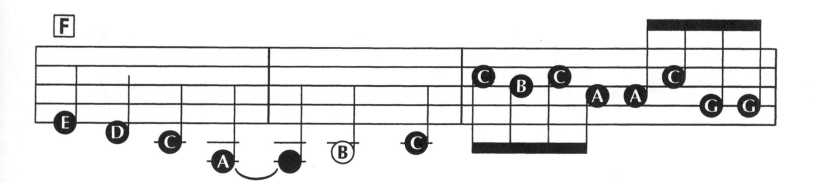

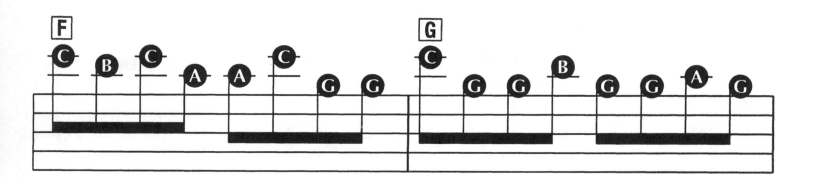

42

D.S. al Coda
(Return to %
Play to ⊕ and
Skip to Coda)

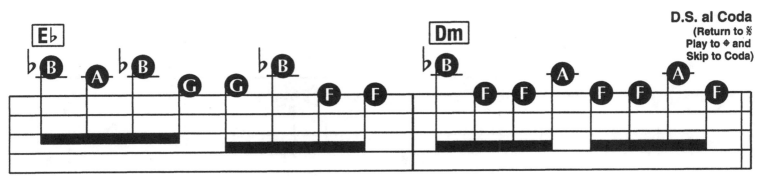

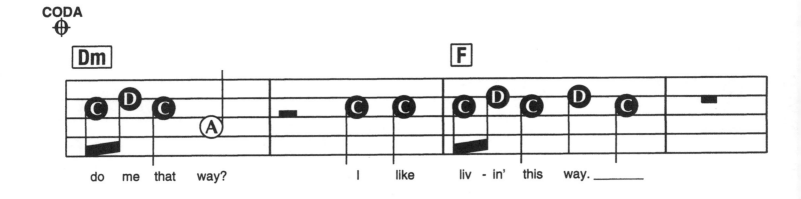

CODA
⊕

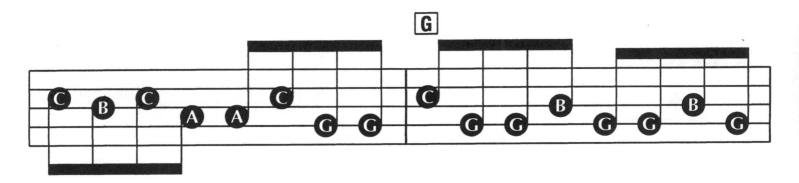

do me that way?     I like liv - in' this way. _____

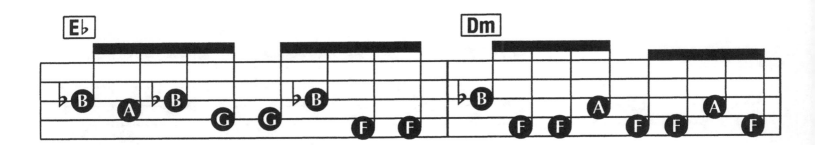

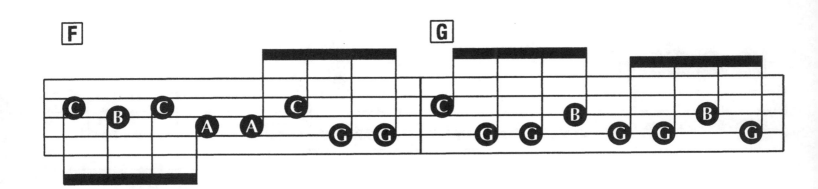

43

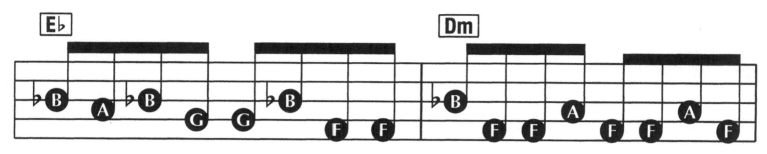

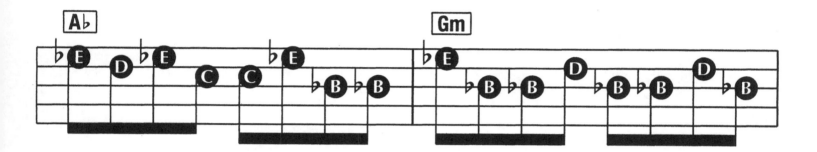

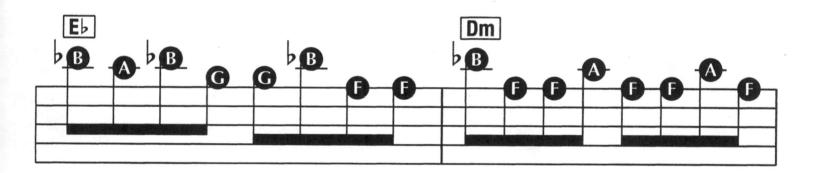

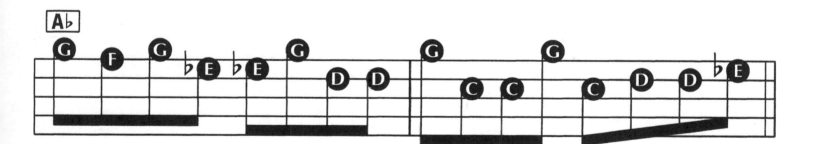

Repeat and Fade

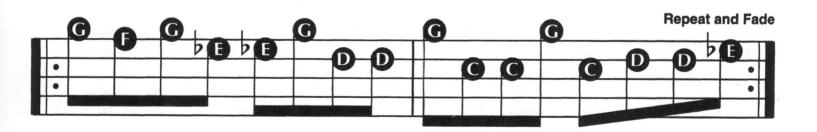

# I Just Can't Stop Loving You

Registration 4
Rhythm: Ballad or Pops

Words and Music by
Michael Jackson

45

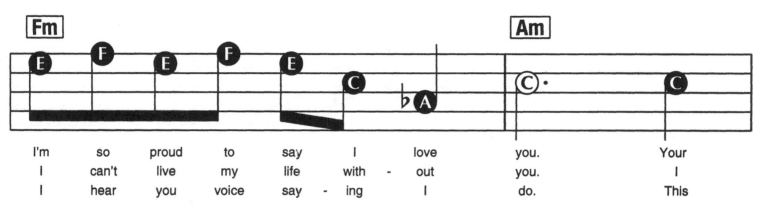

I'm so proud to say I love you. Your
I can't live my life with - out you. I
I hear you voice say - ing I do. This

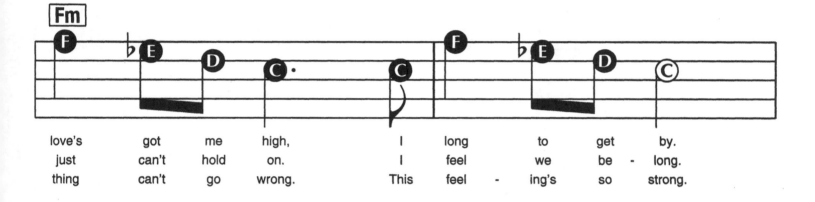

love's got me high, I long to get by.
just can't hold on. I feel we be - long.
thing can't go wrong. This feel - ing's so strong.

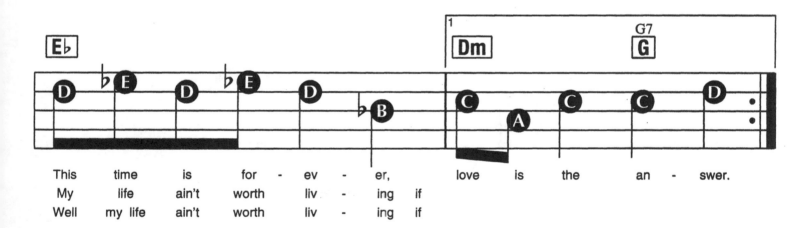

This time is for - ev - er, love is the an - swer.
My life ain't worth liv - ing if
Well my life ain't worth liv - ing if

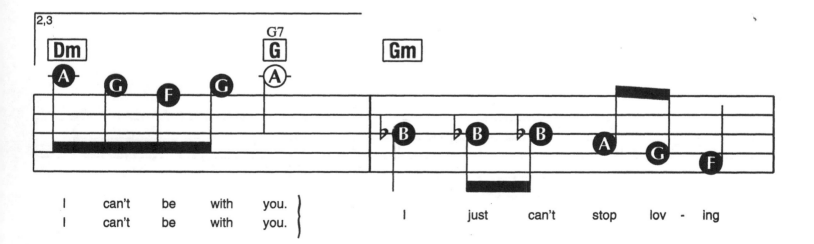

I can't be with you.
I can't be with you.
I just can't stop lov - ing

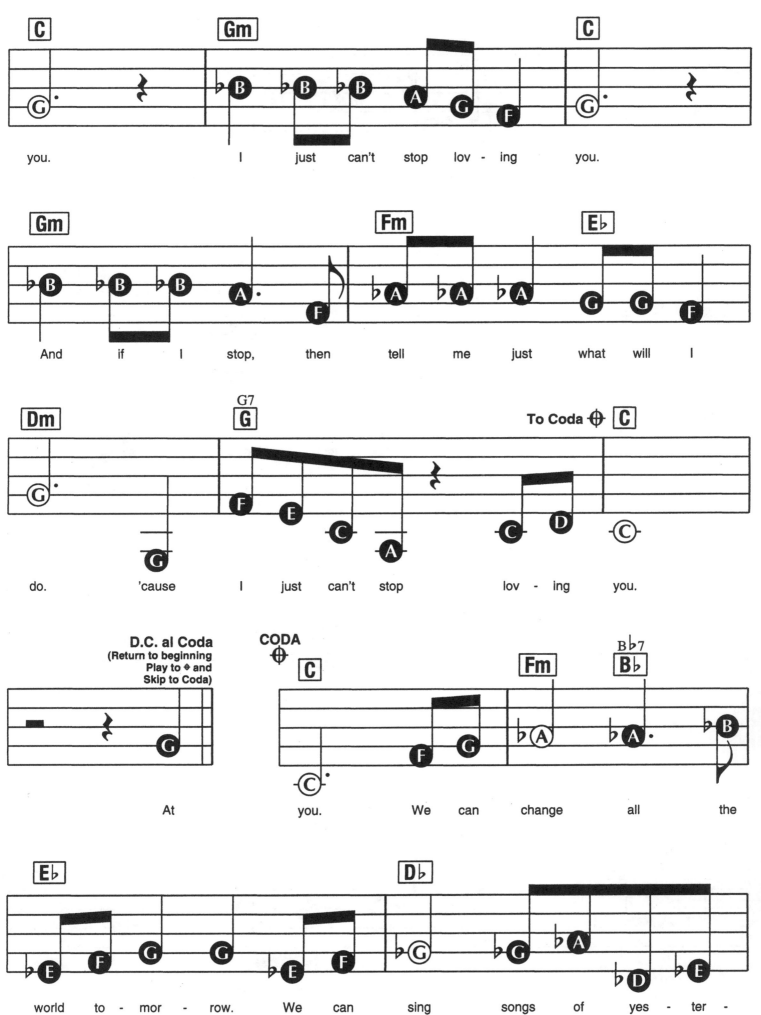

47

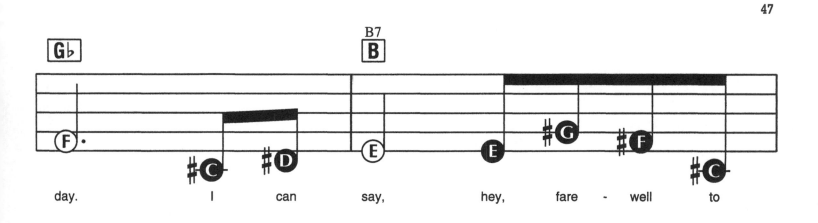

day.   I can say,   hey, fare - well to

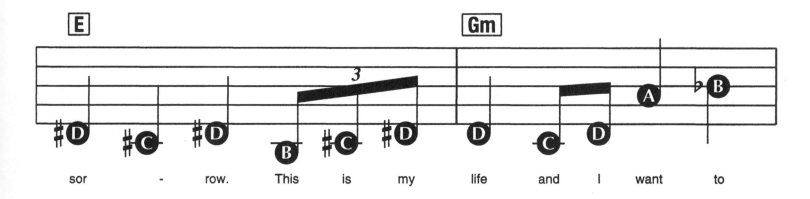

sor - row.   This is my   life and I want to

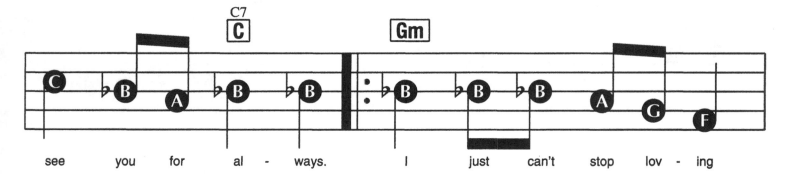

see you for al - ways.   I just can't stop lov - ing

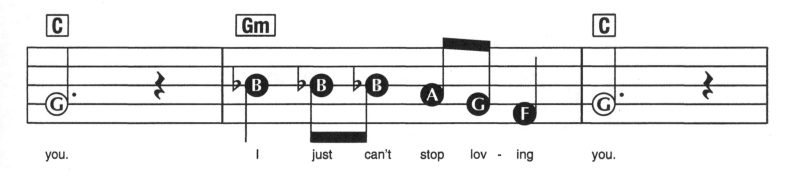

you.   I just can't stop lov - ing you.

**Repeat and Fade**

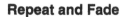

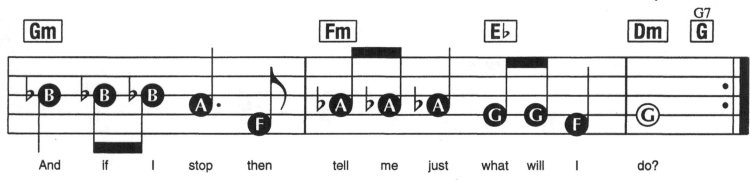

And if I stop then tell me just what will I do?

# Smooth Criminal

Registration 8
Rhythm: Funk or Rock

Words and Music by
Michael Jackson

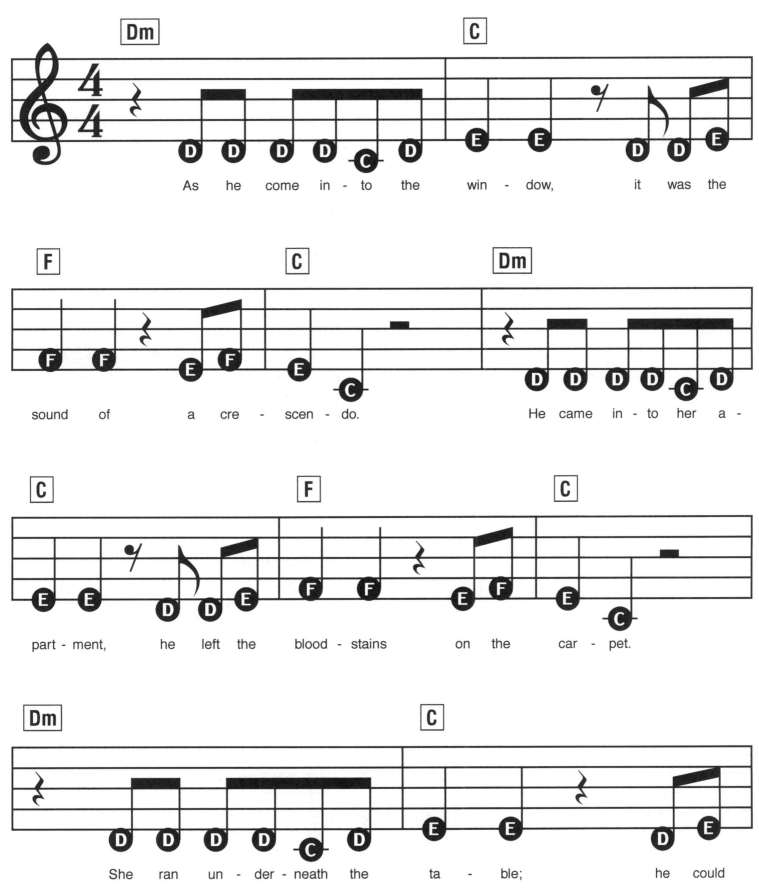

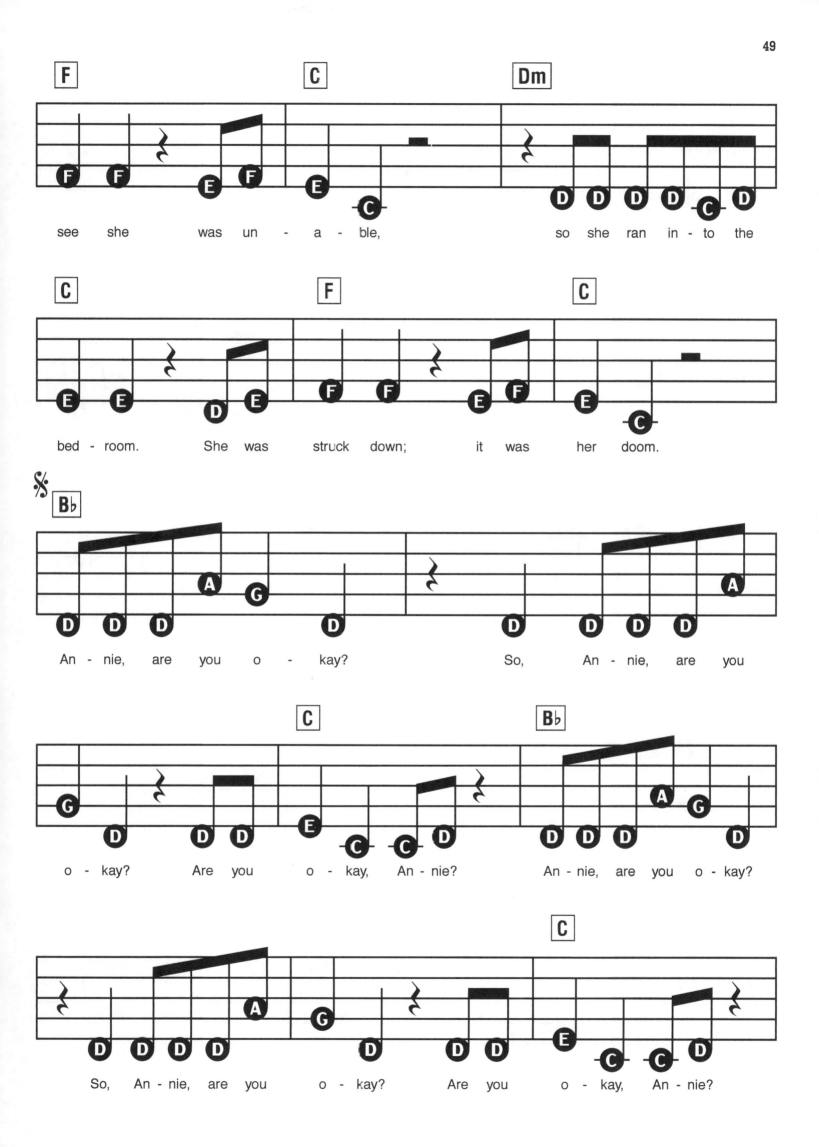

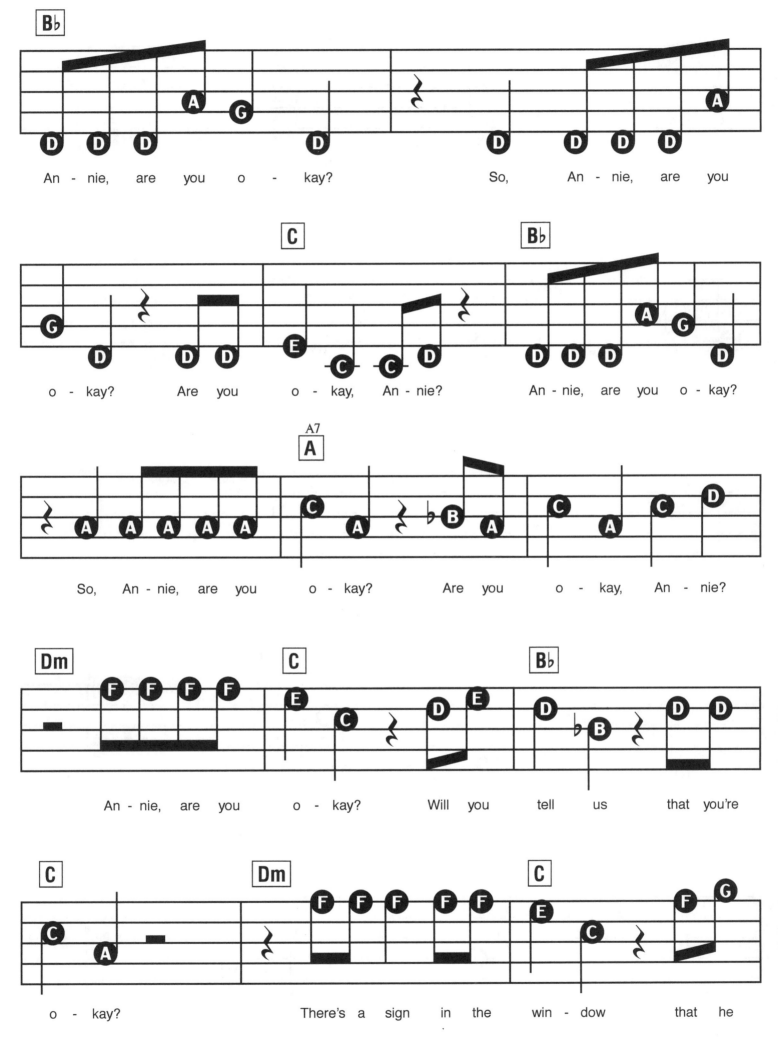

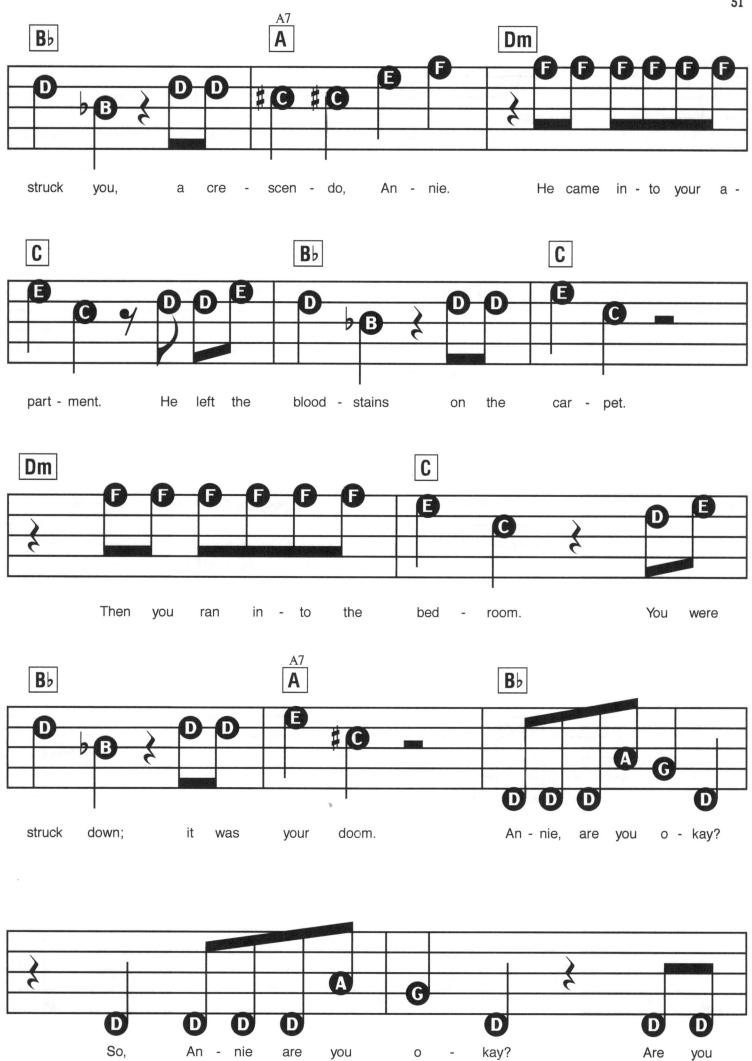

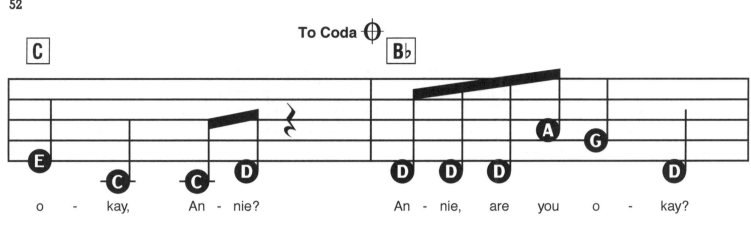

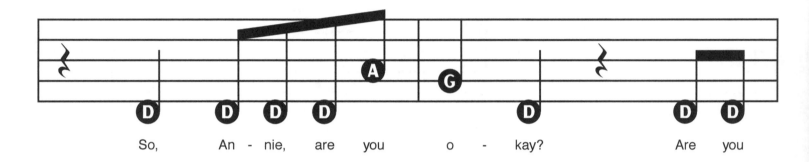

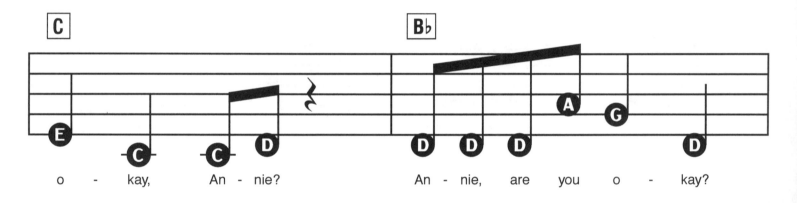

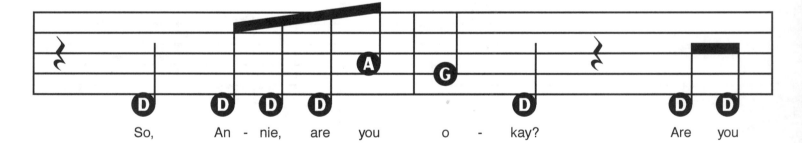

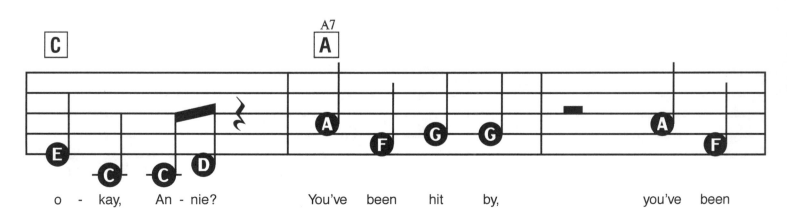

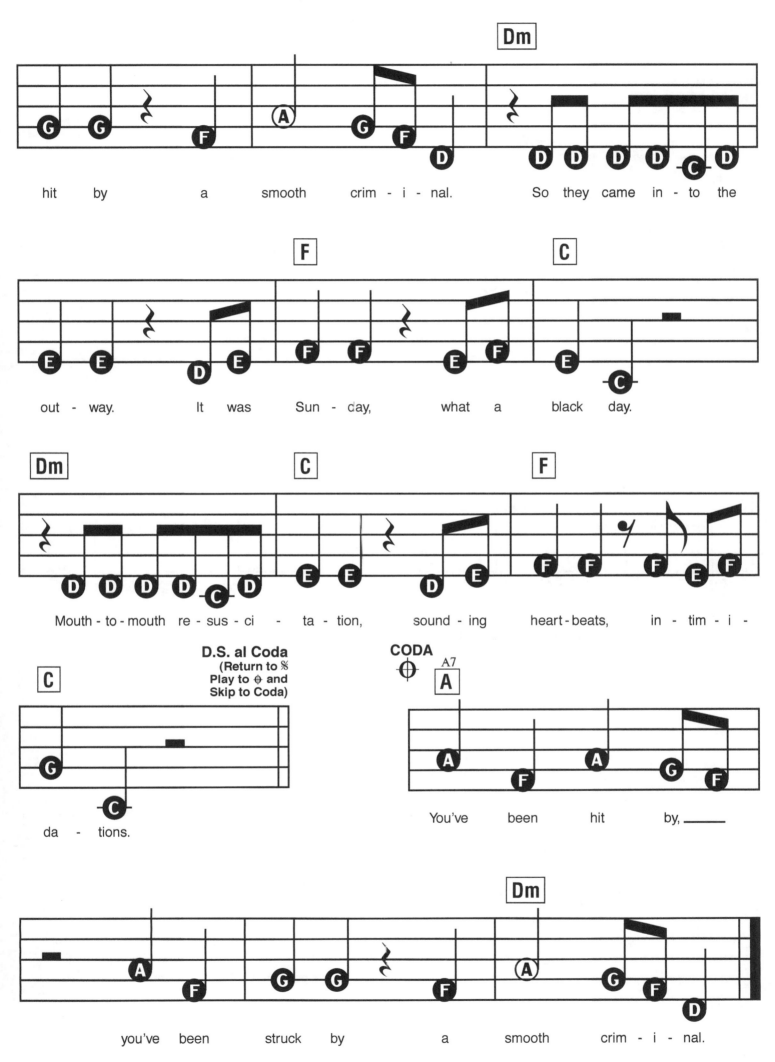

# Thriller

Registration 4
Rhythm: Disco

Words and Music by
Rod Temperton

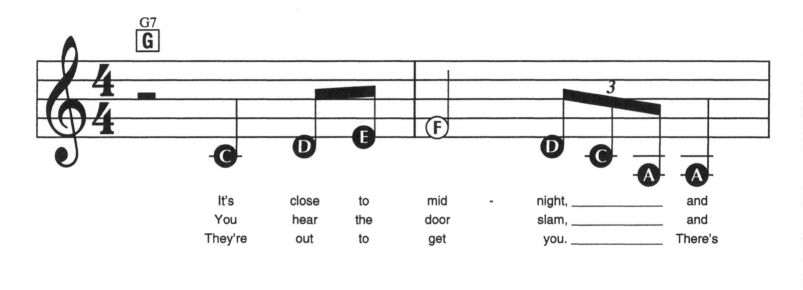

It's close to mid - night, _____ and
You hear the door slam, _____ and
They're out to get you. _____ There's

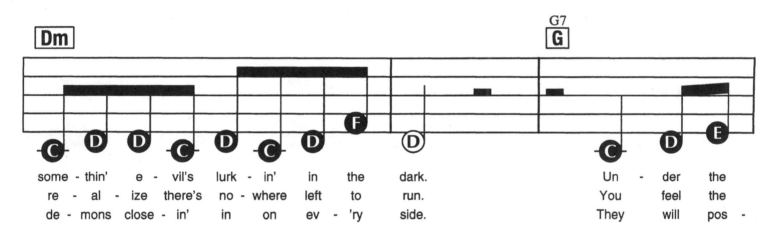

some - thin' e - vil's lurk - in' in the dark. Un - der the
re - al - ize there's no - where left to run. You feel the
de - mons close - in' in on ev - 'ry side. They will pos -

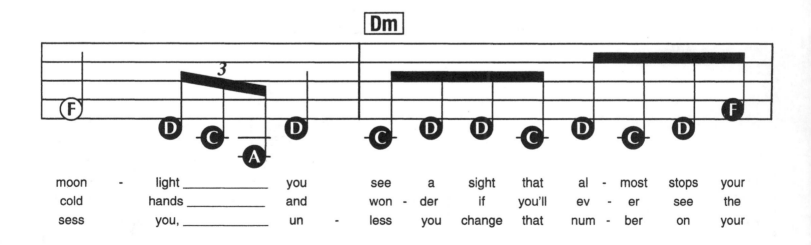

moon - light _____ you see a sight that al - most stops your
cold hands _____ and won - der if you'll ev - er see the
sess you, _____ un - less you change that num - ber on your

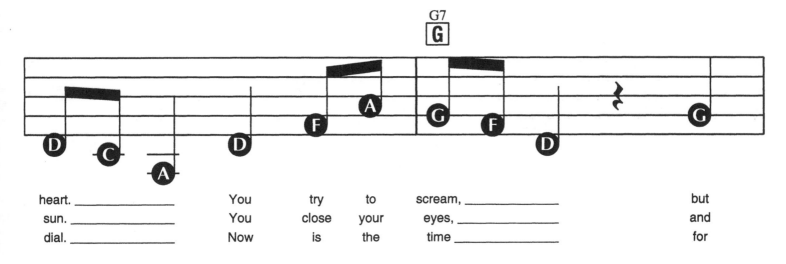

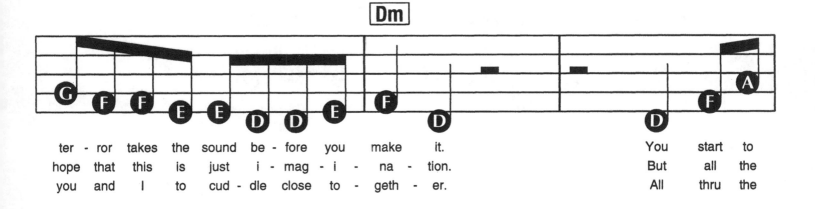

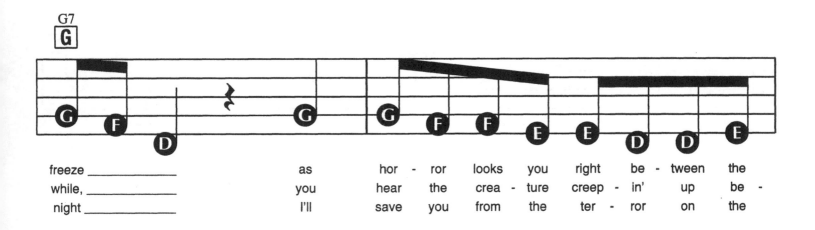

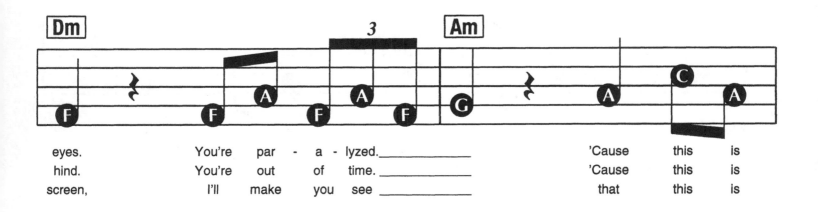

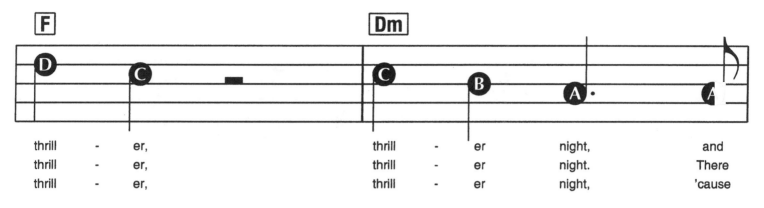

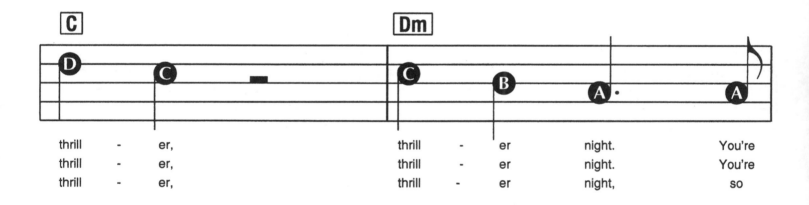

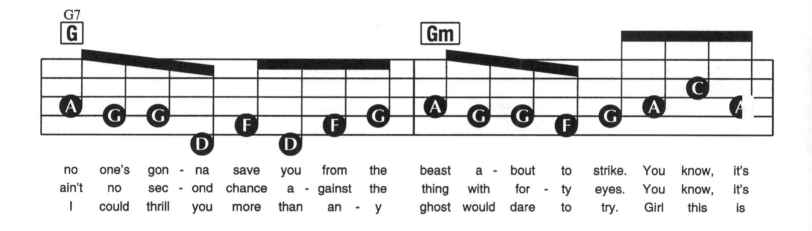

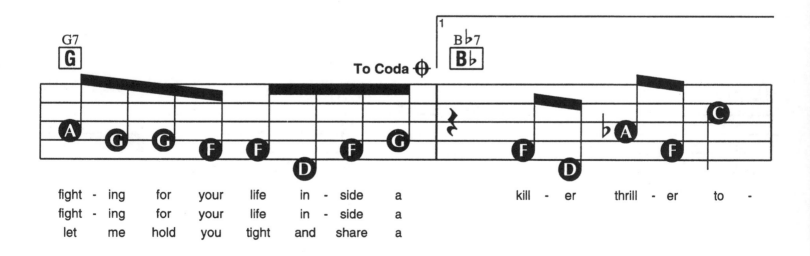

57

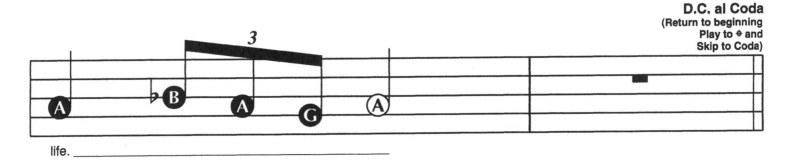

**D.C. al Coda**
(Return to beginning
Play to ◈ and
Skip to Coda)

life. _____

**CODA**

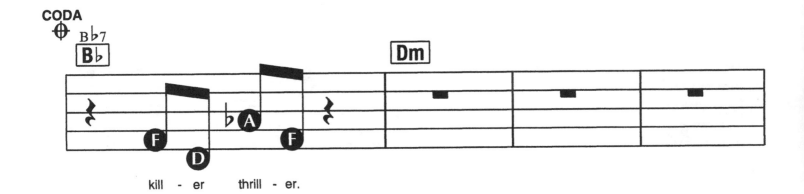

kill - er    thrill - er.

**Repeat ad lib. for rap**

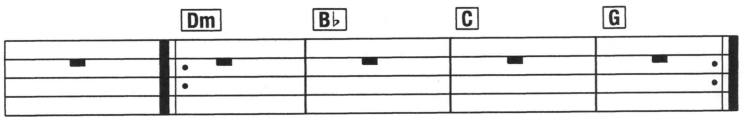

Darkness falls across the land
The midnight hour is close at hand.
Creatures crawl in search of blood
To terrorize y'awl's neighborhood.

And whosoever shall be found
Without the soul for getting down
Must stand and face the hounds of hell
And rot inside a corpse's shell.

The foulest stench is in the air,
The funk of forthy thousand years,
And grizzly ghouls from every tomb
Are closing to seal your doom.

And through the fight to stay alive,
Your body starts to shiver,
For no mere mortal can resist
The evil of a thriller.

# Rock with You

Registration 2
Rhythm: Rock

Words and Music by
Rod Temperton

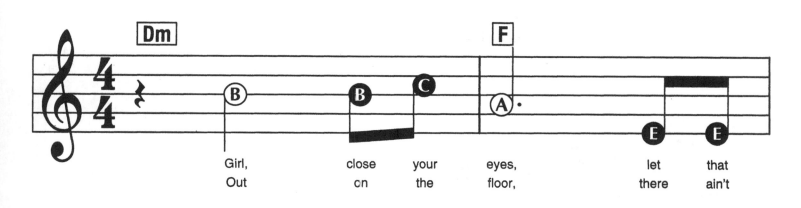

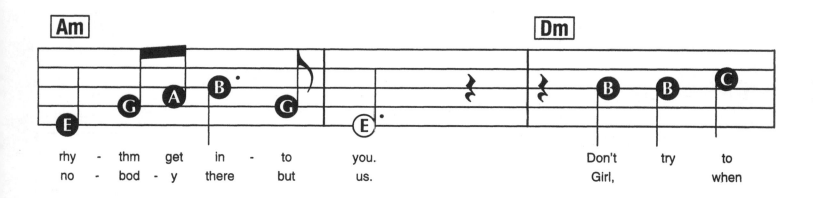

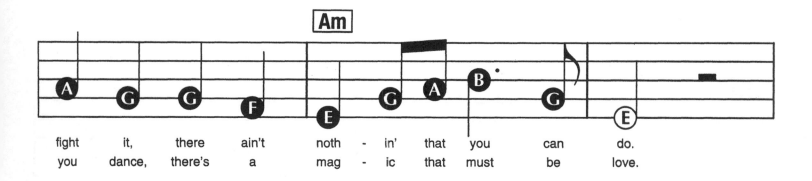

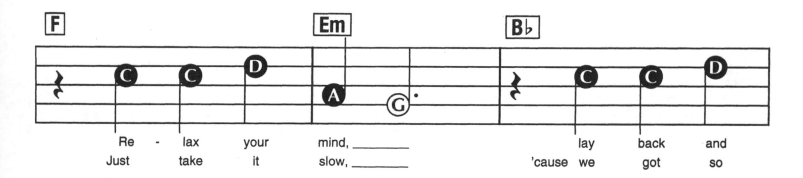

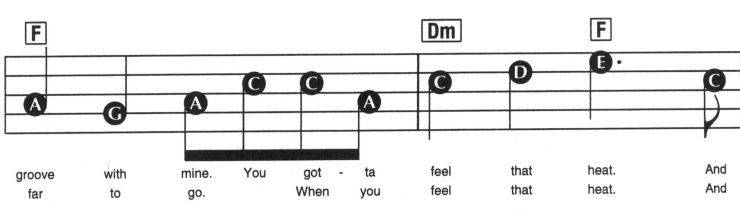

groove with mine. You got - ta feel that heat. And
far to go. When you feel feel that heat. And

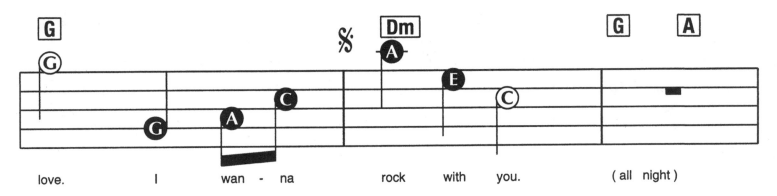

we can ride the boog - ie, share that beat of
we're gonna ride the boog - ie, share that beat of

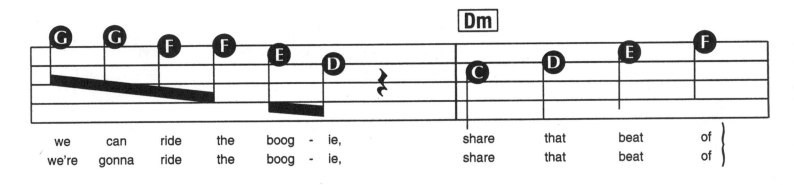

love. I wan - na rock with you. ( all night )

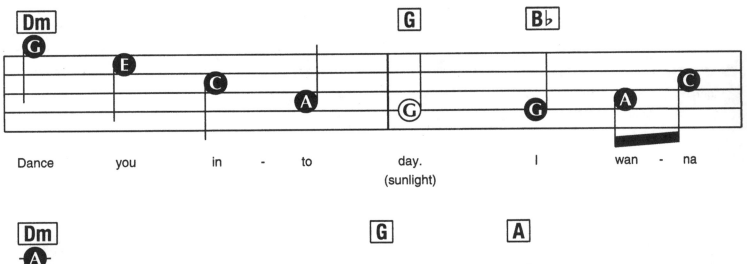

Dance you in - to day. I wan - na
(sunlight)

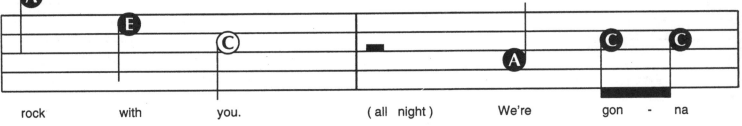

rock with you. ( all night ) We're gon - na

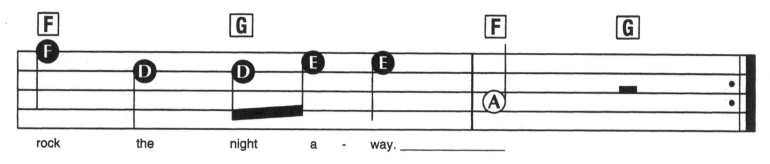

rock          the          night          a -          way. _____

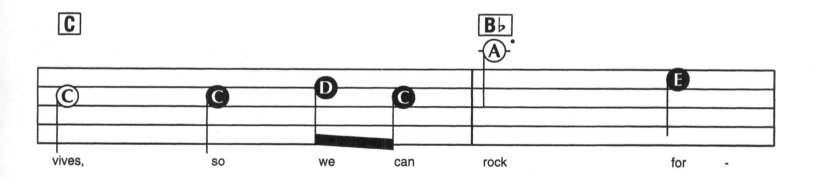

And          when          the          groove          is          dead          and

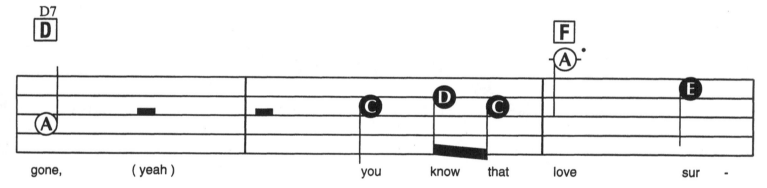

gone,          ( yeah )                    you          know          that          love          sur -

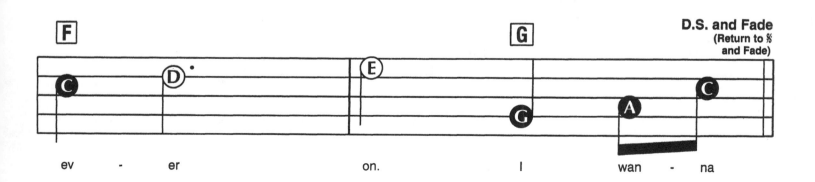

vives,          so          we          can          rock          for -

**D.S. and Fade**
(Return to %
and Fade)

ev - er                    on.          I          wan - na

# Wanna Be Startin' Somethin'

Registration 3
Rhythm: Disco

Words and Music by
Michael Jackson

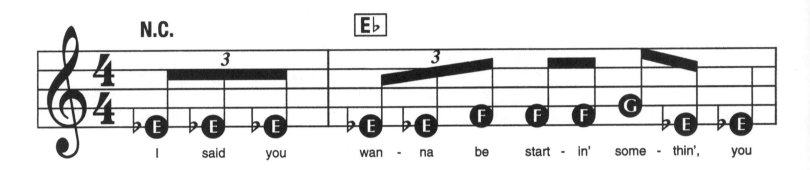

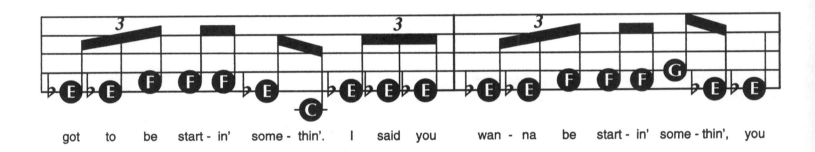

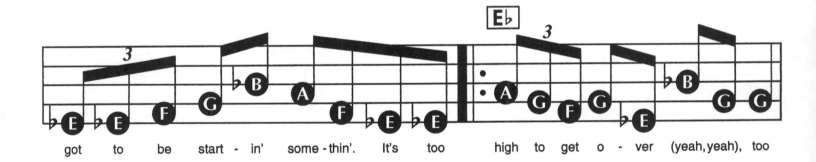

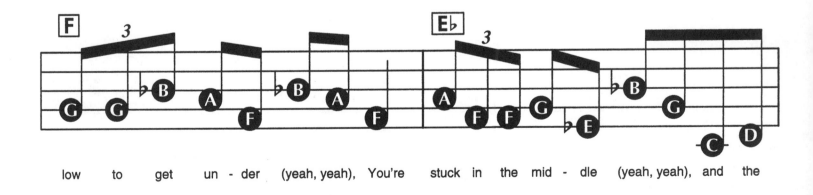

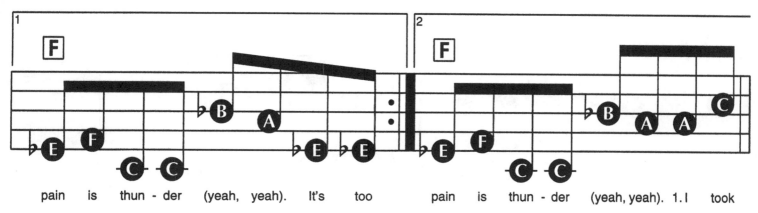

pain is thun - der (yeah, yeah). It's too

pain is thun - der (yeah, yeah). 1. I took

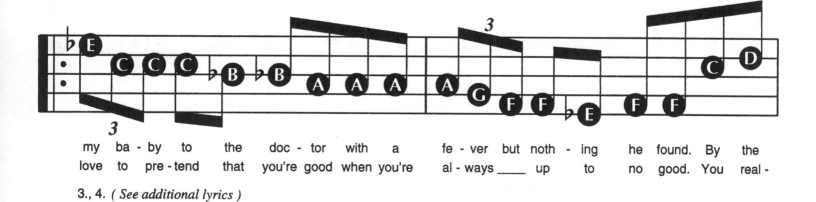

my ba - by to the doc - tor with a fe - ver but noth - ing he found. By the

love to pre - tend that you're good when you're al - ways ____ up to no good. You real -

3., 4. *( See additional lyrics )*

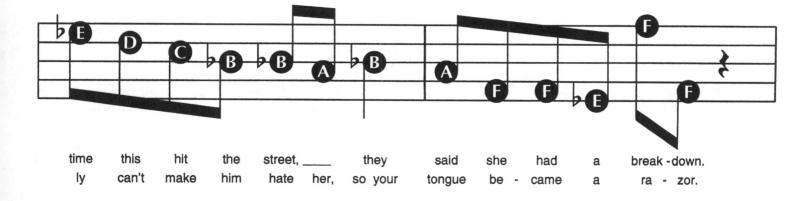

time this hit the street, ____ they said she had a break -down.

ly can't make him hate her, so your tongue be - came a ra - zor.

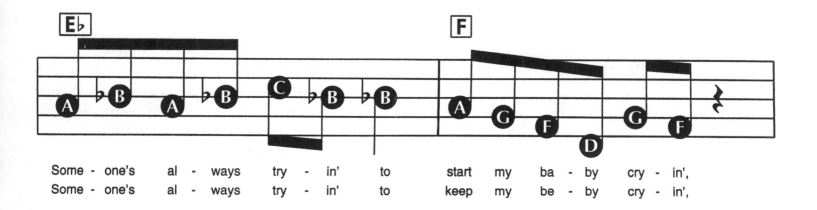

Some - one's al - ways try - in' to start my ba - by cry - in',

Some - one's al - ways try - in' to keep my be - by cry - in',

64

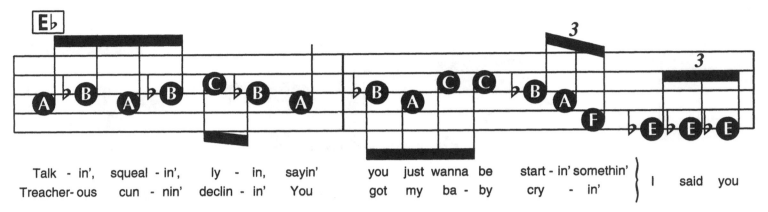

Talk - in', squeal - in', ly - in, sayin'  you just wanna be start - in' somethin' } I said you
Treacher- ous cun - nin' declin - in' You  got my ba - by cry - in'

**Chorus**

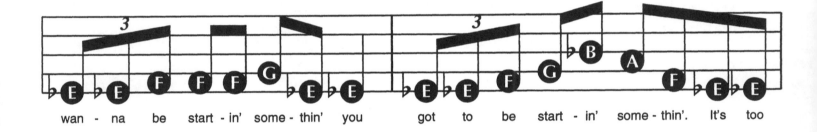

wan - na be start - in' some - thin', you  got to be start - in' some - thin'. I said you

wan - na be start - in' some - thin' you  got to be start - in' some - thin'. It's too

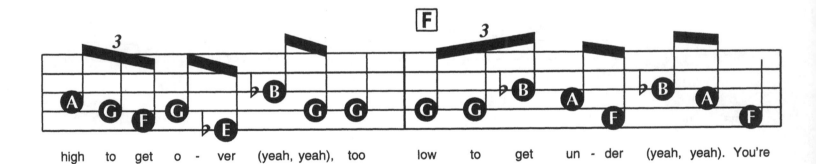

high to get o - ver (yeah, yeah), too  low to get un - der (yeah, yeah). You're

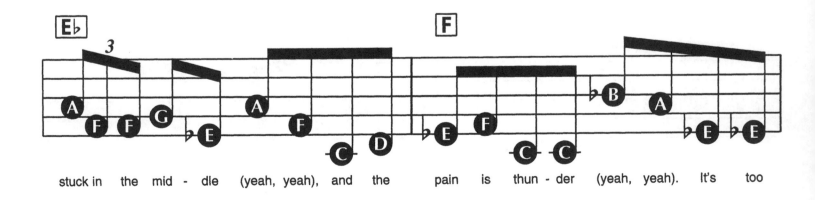

stuck in the mid - dle (yeah, yeah), and the  pain is thun - der (yeah, yeah). It's too

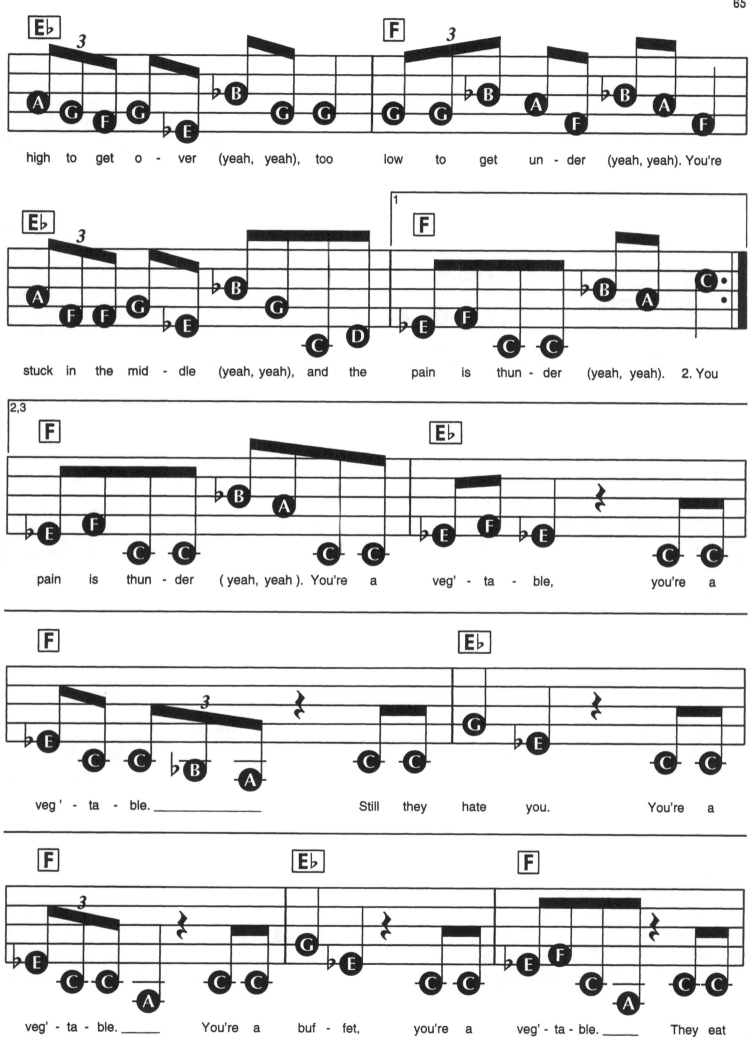

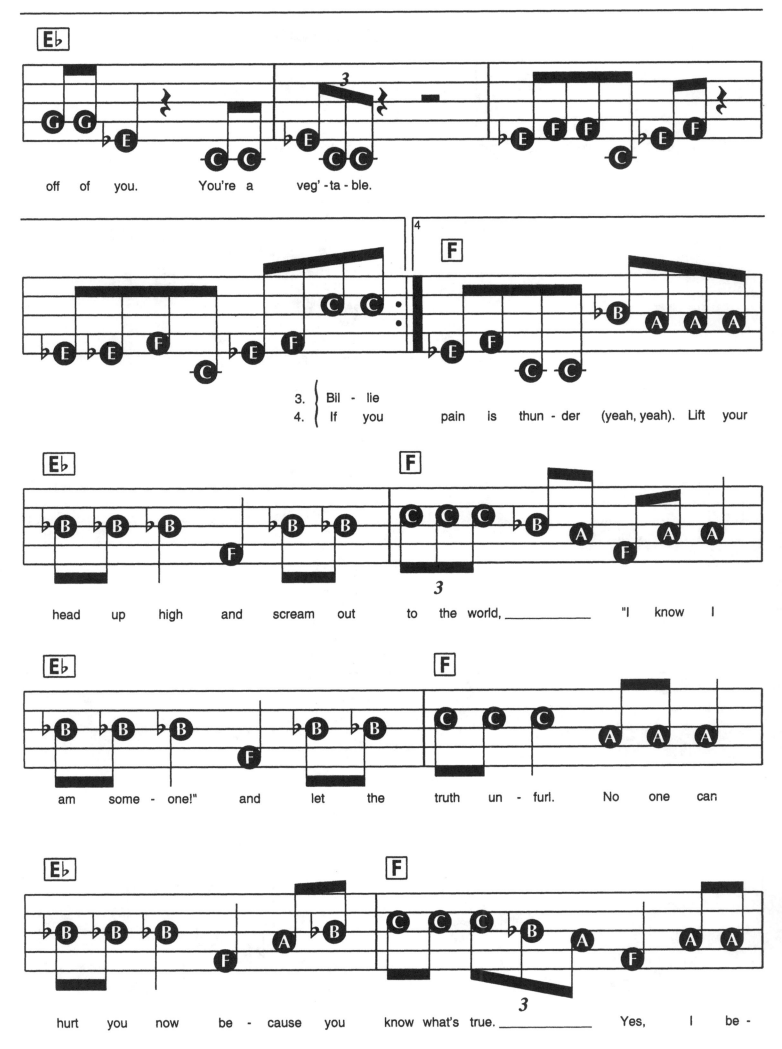

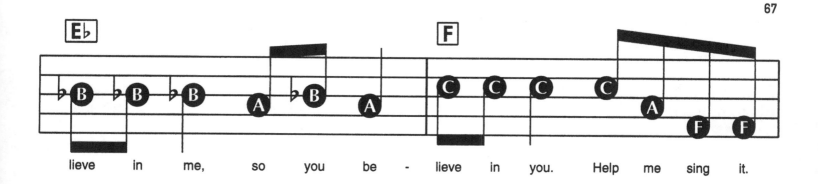

lieve in me, so you be - lieve in you. Help me sing it.

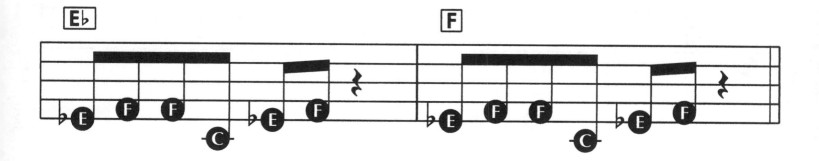

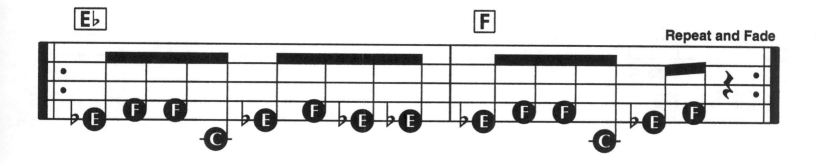

Repeat and Fade

*Additional Lyrics*

3. Billie Jean is always talkin'
   When nobody else is talkin',
   Tellin' lies and rubbin' shoulders,
   So they call her mouth a motor.
   Someone's always tryin'
   To start my baby cryin'
   Talkin', squealin', spyin', sayin' you
   just wanna be startin' somethin'
   I said you

   ( CHORUS )

4. If you can't feed your baby
   Then don't have a baby.
   And don't think maybe,
   If you can't feed your baby.
   You'll be always tryin'
   To stop the child from cryin'
   Nustiln', stealin', lyin'.
   Now baby's slowly dyin'.
   I said you

   ( CHORUS )

# The Way You Make Me Feel

Registration 4
Rhythm: Rock

Words and Music by
Michael Jackson

G  F  G  F

Hey,    pret - ty   ba - by   with   the   high   heels_____   on,
I      like   the   feel - in'   you're   giv - in'_____   me,

G  F  G  F

you    give   me   fev - er   like   I've   nev - er,   ev - er   known.
just   hold   me   ba - by,   and_____   I'm   in   ec - sta - sy.

G  F  G  F  G  F

You're    just   a   prod - uct   of   love - li - ness,   I   like   the   groove   of   your
Oh,       I'll   be   work - in'   from   nine   to   five,   to   buy   you   things_____   to

G  F  C  Bb  C  Bb

walk,   your   talk,   your   dress.   I   feel   your   fev - er   from   miles   a - round.
keep    you   by   my   side.   I   nev - er   felt   so   in   love   be - fore.

# E-Z PLAY® TODAY PUBLICATIONS

*The E-Z Play® Today songbook series is the shortest distance between beginning music and playing fun! Check out this list of highlights and visit www.halleonard.com for a complete listing of all volumes and songlists.*

**HAL•LEONARD®**

Prices, contents, and availability subject to change without notice.